With
JOHN BURROUGHS
in Field and Wood

With
JOHN BURROUGHS
in Field and Wood

EDITED AND ILLUSTRATED

BY

Elizabeth Burroughs Kelley

South Brunswick and New York: A. S. Barnes and Co.
London: Thomas Yoseloff Ltd

A. S. Barnes and Co., Inc.
Cranbury, New Jersey 08512

Thomas Yoseloff Ltd
108 New Bond Street
London W1Y OQK, England

SBN
498 06892 7
Printed in the United States of America

To Ursula and John, my sister and
brother, and to Stacy Burroughs
Chamberlin and all the children who
have had happy days at Riverby.

Foreword

Few American writers have been so well loved as John Burroughs and probably no one has had more influence in creating a popular interest in nature. Today nature study is so much a part of our everyday life we are apt to take it for granted, but when John Burroughs began to write about birds, shortly after the Civil War, there were no bird guides, no nature magazines, nor any nature clubs. Through his books, of which nearly a million and a half copies were sold during his lifetime, an interest in outdoor life was started that soon became widespread, for his essays made others see what pleasure they too could have in learning about the world of field and wood. "The gospel of my books," he once said, "if they have any gospel is to see the wonderful and beautiful in the simple things all around you."

The first chapter in this book gives a short sketch of his life; the others tell of some of his observations and experiences. The selections have been taken from his books as follows: "Near Views of Wild Life," *Squirrels and Other Fur-Bearers* and *Under The Apple Trees;* "Camping with President Roosevelt," *Camping and Tramping with Roosevelt;* "Migrating Birds and Bird-Songs," *Field and Study, Signs and Seasons,* and *The Ways of Nature;* "The Pastoral Bees," *Locusts and Wild Honey;* "A Young Marsh Hawk," *Riverby;* "Birds'-Nesting," *Locusts and Wild Honey* and *Field and Study;* "Exploring the Delaware," *Pepacton;* "Bird Neighbors at Slabsides,"

Far and Near; "Slide Mountain," *Riverby;* "A Barn-Door Outlook," *The Summit of the Years;* "The Art of Seeing Things," *Leaf and Tendril, Field and Study, The Summit of the Years,* and *Riverby;* "The Wit of a Duck," *The Ways of Nature;* "The Pleasures of a Naturalist," *Under the Maples* and *Pepacton;* "Wild Life in Winter," *The Ways of Nature, The Summit of the Years, Signs and Seasons, Far and Near,* and *Under the Apple Trees.*

Material from these books written by John Burroughs is reprinted by permission of the publishers Houghton Mifflin Company and Russell and Russell.

With the permission of the New York State Historical Association, Cooperstown, I have used some of the material which appeared in my article "John Burroughs' Student Days at Cooperstown," in the July 1963 issue of *New York History.*

Contents

	Introduction	11
1	Near Views of Wild Life	21
2	Camping with President Roosevelt	31
3	Migrating Birds and Bird-Songs	39
4	The Pastoral Bees	47
5	A Young Marsh Hawk	54
6	Birds'-Nesting	61
7	Exploring the Delaware	73
8	Bird Neighbors at Slabsides	86
9	Slide Mountain	95
10	A Barn-Door Outlook	105
11	The Art of Seeing Things	118
12	The Wit of a Duck	125
13	The Pleasures of a Naturalist	130
14	Wild Life in Winter	138

Introduction

As a boy, John Burroughs had no idea that he would be one of the best known writers of his time, that schools and clubs would be named for him, and that after his death people would be coming from all over the United States to visit his grave.

He was one of ten children, born on a farm fifty miles from the nearest railroad and a dozen miles from the nearest stage coach line, where life was not far removed from that of pioneer days. Both his father and his mother had been born in log cabins.

The house in which he was born, on April 3, 1837, near Roxbury, New York, was an unpainted farmhouse on the side of Old Clump Mountain. The family themselves made much of what they used on the farm and the children were kept so busy with all the chores that their schooling was intermittent and brief.

There was no radio, no television, not even a daily newspaper to keep the family informed, so they knew little of what was going on in the rest of the world. And if they wanted to go anywhere they had to walk or ride in a farm wagon over rough roads at the rate of a few miles an hour. They did, however, have what they called the "pleasure wagon," a three-seated affair that had been made by a local carpenter, but it was generally used only on Sundays and travel wasn't much faster in it. Sometimes when an older boy was courting a girl he might hire a horse and

The Burroughs homestead

buggy to take her riding, but that could not often be
afforded.

Yet the children did have fun even though they all had
to share in the chores on the farm. They made most of
their own toys and invented their own games. Learning to
do things for yourself, as John found out, was an advantage
in growing up on such a farm. It taught him to rely on himself. His ambition, which was shown particularly in the
matter of going to school, was greater than his brothers'.
They all attended the one-room schoolhouse in the next
valley, called West Settlement, but whereas learning to
read and write and do a little arithmetic was enough for

his brothers and sisters, John wanted to go away to school and was willing to work to pay for his tuition.

Though only seventeen, with the help of a doctor the family knew in a neighboring county, he obtained a job teaching a roomful of children in a village called Tongore. Then with what he earned, he was able to attend the Hedding Literary Institute at Ashland in Greene County, New York, for three months. This was a new school (no longer in existence) with a library of fifteen hundred books. Behind the school building was a rock where it is said John Burroughs wrote his first essay.

After more teaching, the following year, he spent three months at the Cooperstown Seminary. This was all he could afford but the importance of those three months in the development of his interests and personality can hardly be overestimated. Consider his background: a boy who had grown up in the hills of Delaware County in a family without interest in books and with the limited schooling of such rural areas might have spent the rest of his life there like his brothers if he had not had that longing to know more about the world.

In the congenial environment of the Seminary, along with his study of Latin, French, English, and mathematics, he did much reading and experimental writing. He developed so rapidly as a writer that he was soon at the top of the Seminary's English Composition class. He also, for the first time, saw himself in print as an author when the Bloomville (Delaware County) *Mirror* accepted for publication an article he had hopefully submitted.

He joined the Seminary's Websterian Society, quickly became one of its leaders, and before the term ended was elected the Society's president. At the Seminary's closing exercises, in the school chapel, he was one of the speakers, an honor he had well earned.

After leaving the Seminary he was again to experience lonely days of teaching in one-room country schools, and discouraging days with financial difficulties, for teachers were poorly paid and his first published articles brought him little money. No one at home had any sympathy with his literary aspirations, nor did the girl he married wish him to continue what to her was profitless scribbling. Yet his success at the Seminary had shown him that he did have ability and he was now determined not to be daunted by discouragements. He knew that he wanted to be an author.

When he was twenty-six he gave up teaching and moved to Washington, D. C., where he found a job as clerk in the Treasury Department, and continued writing in his spare time. He was encouraged by the *Atlantic Monthly,* which had already accepted one of his articles while he was still teaching, and wrote his first book about a friend he made in Washington—the poet Walt Whitman.

John Burroughs might have been just another essayist, critic, and biographer if, shortly before coming to Washington, he had not seen Audubon's *Birds of America.* As a boy growing up on the farm he had been interested in birds and enjoyed watching them. Now he took up bird-study with zest, however since little had been written about them he had much to learn for himself. There was Alexander Wilson's Ornithology, published in nine volumes from 1808 to 1814, and also Audubon's, but these folio-size, expensive books were not generally available for the public.

At first the thought of writing essays about birds did not occur to him, but his bird-study gave him so much pleasure he decided to share it with others and so wrote "With the Birds," an article which the *Atlantic Monthly* accepted. When he had enough essays to fill a book, he published them in a volume called *Wake-Robin,* "the common name of the white trillium, which blooms in all our woods, and which marks the arrival of all our birds." This book was an immediate success and so he went on to write others.

Meanwhile he had been given a number of promotions in the Treasury Department until he was now Chief in the Organization Division in the Bureau of National Banks. He was also sent to England on official business for the Department and spent several weeks abroad with all his expenses paid. But uppermost in his mind was a literary career, so after nine years in Washington he resigned to accept a job as special National Bank Examiner for districts that included those along the Hudson River since this would allow him more free time for writing.

Financial worries now over, he looked for a place on the Hudson to make his permanent home and selected a fruit farm at West Park, half way between Albany and New York, on the West side of the river, which he named Riverby. Here he and his wife, Ursula North, built a handsome stone house. It was lonely here at first, after the bustling life of the Capital, especially so for his wife since he spent much of his time out-of-doors, exploring the countryside around his new home, thereby obtaining material for further essays.

He did not go out, however, with the purpose of writing something and he never took a notebook. What he preferred to do was to let the experience become part of his thought and feeling, and wait to write about it until the relatively insignificant details had been forgotten. As he explained in his Introduction to *Wake-Robin:* "If I name every bird I see in my walk, describe its color and ways, etc., give a lot of facts or details about the bird, it is doubtful that my reader is interested. But if I relate the bird in some way to human life, to my own life—show what it is to me and what it is in the landscape and the season,—then do I give my reader a live bird and not a labeled specimen." He wanted his readers to know, moreover, that what he wrote "was a careful and conscientious record of actual observations and experiences." He took no liberties with facts nor did he let his imagination influence him to the extent of giving a false impression though he did have a poet's imagination.

He also had a sense of humor and an engaging style so that in writing up his experiences he made them sound so enjoyable that readers wanted to have similar experiences. It was a new type of essay as nothing quite like this had been done before, and he soon had a large popular following—some of his essays were used for nature-study in schools, John Burroughs Clubs were formed for adult groups, and many of his readers corresponded with him and came to see him. Today there are numerous writers contributing nature articles to magazines, but John Burroughs, pioneer in this field, launched the movement which every year takes thousands of people out-of-doors looking for birds and finding new pleasure in the study of nature.

Among those who came to see him were prominent people of his day, including Theodore Roosevelt, President of the United States. For some of his entertaining he built a slab-covered cabin about a mile and a half from his home. "Slabsides," as he called the cabin, with its big stone fireplace and handcrafted furnishings, was set in the woods and not far from a beautiful stream. Here school children, college students, club members, some in groups and some individually, came to see him, talk to him, and be taken on nature walks. There also were special visitors such as John Muir and Henry Ford and many other friends.

When John Burroughs's son Julian was growing up, he used to share many of his adventures with him. They went swimming, skating, boating, fishing, hiking, and camping together. John Burroughs was the sort of man that people enjoyed being with—he had so many invitations that I sometimes wonder how he managed to do as much writing as he did.

Not all that he wrote was on nature. He also wrote on

some aspects of philosophy and of scientific study; he wrote poetry, and about a third dealt with the field of literary criticism. His best known poem is *Waiting*, which has been an inspiration to many people in the hundred years since it was written. He was only twenty-five years old when he wrote *Waiting*, and was going through a period of discouragement, but in the poem he expresses the belief that his aspirations would yet be achieved.

In his later years he fixed up a farmhouse which had been built by one of his brothers on the edge of the Burroughs farm at Roxbury, and here he spent his summers and continued his writing right up to the end of his long life. Today Woodchuck Lodge, which he appropriately named the farmhouse, has now been designated a National Historic Landmark.

John Burroughs, who died on March 29, 1921, was buried, as he requested, in a field above Woodchuck Lodge. His body lies near a large boulder on which, as a boy, he used to sit after the day's work was done and, looking out over the mountains, dream of what life might hold in store for him.

Elizabeth Burroughs Kelley

With
JOHN BURROUGHS
in Field and Wood

1

Near Views of Wild Life

[In his walks through field and wood, John Burroughs used to enjoy studying tracks in the snow, for sometimes they told a story. Here is an instance:]

In walking through the woods one day in early winter, we read upon the newly fallen snow the record of a mink's fright the night before. The mink had been traveling through the woods post-haste, not along the watercourses where one sees them by day, but over ridges and across valleys. We followed his track some distance to see what adventures he had met with. We tracked him through a bushy swamp, and saw where he had left it to explore a pile of rocks, then where he had taken to the swamp again, and where he had entered the more open woods. Presently the track turned sharply about, and doubled upon itself in long hurried strides. What caused the mink to change his mind so suddenly?

We explored a few paces ahead and came upon a fox-track. The mink had probably seen the fox stalking stealthily through the woods, and the sight had doubtless brought his heart into his mouth. I think he climbed a tree, and waited till the fox had passed. His track disappeared amid a clump of hemlocks, and then reappeared again a little beyond them. It described a big loop around, then crossed the fox track only a few yards from the point where its course was interrupted. Then it followed a little watercourse, went under a rude bridge in a wood-road, then mingled with squirrel tracks in a denser part of the thicket.

You may know the mink's track upon the snow from those of the squirrel's at once. In the squirrel-track the prints of the large hind feet are ahead, with the prints of the smaller fore feet just behind them, as in the case of the rabbit. The mink, in running, usually plants his hind feet exactly upon the track of his fore feet, and closer together than the squirrel. One winter day I had a good view of a mink running upon the snow and ice along the edge of a stream. He had seen or heard me, and was making a little extra speed. He bounded along with his back much arched, in a curiously stiff and mechanical sort of way, with none of the grace and ease of the squirrel. He leaped high, and cleared about two and a half feet at a bound.

In February a new track appears upon the snow, slender and delicate, about a third larger than that of the gray squirrel, indicating no haste or speed, but, on the contrary, denoting the most imperturbable ease and leisure, the footprints so close together that the trail appears like a chain of curiously carved links. Sir *Mephitis mephitica*, or, in plain English, the skunk, has waked up from his six weeks' nap, and come out into society again. There is no such word as hurry in his dictionary, as you may see by his path upon the snow.

He has a secret to keep and knows it, and is careful not to betray himself until he can do so with the most telling effect. I have known him to preserve his serenity even when caught in a steel trap, and look the very picture of injured innocence, manoeuvering carefully and deliberately to extricate his foot from the grasp of the naughty jaws. Do not by any means take pity on him, and lend a helping hand.

The skunk visits every farm sooner or later. One night I came near shaking hands with one on my very door-stone. I thought it was the cat, and put down my hand to stroke it, when the creature, probably appreciating my mistake, moved off up the bank, revealing to me the white stripe on its body and the kind of cat I had saluted.

[John Burroughs was interested to learn whether it is true that a skunk, when held upside down by the tail, cannot use its weapon. Just holding a skunk's tail down with a stick is not effective, so he found out with unpleasant results. But he did succeed another time and he had his son photograph him holding the skunk head downward. Of course he did not walk up to the skunk and grab its tail. He found it caught by its foot in a trap and by careful manoeuvring managed to get hold of the tail before the animal was in position to act.

About this experience he wrote: "I did something the other day with a wild animal that I had never done before or seen done, though I had heard of it: I carried a live skunk by its tail and there was 'nothing doing,' as the boys say. I did not have to bury my clothes. I knew from observation that the skunk could not use its battery with effect without throwing its tail over its back. Therefore, for once at least, I had the courage of my convictions and verified the fact."]

Red and gray squirrels are more or less active all winter, though very shy, and, I am inclined to think, partially nocturnal in their habits. Here a gray one has just passed— came down that tree and went up this; there he dug for a beechnut, and left the burr on the snow. How did he know where to dig? The red squirrel lays up no stores like the provident chipmunk, but scours about for food in all weathers, feeding upon the seeds in the cones of the hemlock that still cling to the tree, upon sumac-bobs, and the seeds of frozen apples.

A hard winter affects the chipmunks very little; they

are snug and warm in their burrows in the ground and under the rocks, with a bountiful store of nuts or grain. I have heard of nearly a half-bushel of chestnuts being taken from a single den. They usually hole up in November, and do not come out again till March or April unless the winter is very open and mild. Hence, when the chipmunk emerges in March and is seen upon his little journeys along the fences, or perched upon a log or rock near his hole in the woods, it is another sign that spring is at hand. His store of nuts may or may not be all consumed; it is certain that he is no sluggard, to sleep away these first bright warm days.

[At Woodchuck Lodge John Burroughs had a pet chipmunk about which he wrote in *Under the Apple Trees*. Sitting by the open door of his hay-barn study near the orchard, he watched Mr. Chipmunk daily.]

When the chipmunk is in the open, the sense of danger is never absent from him. He is always on the alert. In his excursions along the fences to collect wild buckwheat, wild cherries, and various grains, he is watchfulness itself. In every trip to his den with his supplies, his manner is like that of the baseball-player in running bases—he makes a dash from my study, leaping high over the grass and weeds, to an apple-tree ten yards away; here he pauses a few seconds and nervously surveys his course ahead; then he makes another sprint to a second apple-tree, and pauses as before, quickly glancing round; then in a few leaps he is at home, and in his den. Returning, he usually pursues the same course. He leaves no trail, and is never off his guard. No baseball runner was ever more watchful. Apparently while in the open he does not draw one breath free from a keen sense of danger.

I have tempted him to search my coat pockets for the nuts or cherry-pits that I have placed there, and, when he does so, he seems to appreciate at what a disadvantage his enemy might find him—his eyes are for the moment cov-

Woodchuck Lodge

ered, his rear is exposed, his whole situation is very in-
secure; hence he seizes a nut and reverses his position in
a twinkling; his body palpitates; his eyes bulge; then he
dives in again and seizes another nut as before, acting as
if he thought each moment might be his last. When he
goes into the tin cocoa-box for the cherry-pits, he does it
with the hurry of fear; his eyes are above the rim every
second or two; he does not stop to clean the pits as he
does when on my table, but scoops them up with the greatest precipitation, as if he feared I might clap on the lid
at any moment and make him prisoner.

In all the hundred and one trips he has made from my
study to his den he has not for one moment forgotten himself; he runs all the bases with the same alertness and pre-

caution. Coming back, he emerges from his hole, sits up, washes his face, then looks swiftly about, and is off for the base of supplies.

I can talk to my chipmunk in low, slow tones and he heeds me not, but any unusual sound outside the study, and he is alertness itself. One day when he was on my table a crow flew over and called sharply and loudly; the chipmunk sat up and took notice instantly; with his paws upon his breast he listened and looked intently for a few seconds, and then resumed his foraging. At another time the sharp call of a red squirrel in a tree near by made him still more nervous. With one raised paw he looked and listened for two or three minutes. The red squirrel hazes him on all occasions, and, I think, often robs him of his stores.

He has at last become so familiar that he climbs to my lap, then to the table, then to my shoulder and head, looking for the kernels of popcorn that he is convinced have some perennial source of supply near me or about me. He clears up every kernel, and then on his return, in a few minutes, there they are again! I might think him a good deal puzzled by the prompt renewal of the supply if I were to read my own thoughts into his little noddle, but I see he is only eager to gather his harvest while it is plentiful and so near at hand. No, he is not influenced even by that consideration; he does not consider at all, in fact, he just goes for the corn in eagerness and haste.

Yet, if he does not reflect, he certainly has a wisdom and foresight of his own. This morning I mixed kernels of fresh-cut green corn with a handful of the dry, hard popcorn upon the floor. At first he began to eat the soft sweet corn, but, finding the small, dry kernels of the popcorn, he at once began to stuff his cheek pockets with them, and when they were full he hastened off to his den. Back he came in about three minutes and he kept on doing this till the popcorn was all gone; then he proceeded to make his breakfast off the green corn.

When this was exhausted, he began to strip some choke-cherries (which I had also placed among the corn) of their skins and pulp, and to fill his pockets with the pits, thus carrying no perishable food to his den. He acted exactly as if he knew that the green corn and the choke-cherries would spoil in his underground retreat, and that the hard, dry kind, and the cherry-pits, would keep. He did know it, but not as you and I know it, by experience; he knew it, as all the wild creatures know how to get on in the world, by the wisdom that pervades nature, and is much older than we or they are.

My chipmunk knows corn, cherry-pits, buckwheat, beech-nuts, apple-seeds, and probably several other foods, at sight; but peach-pits, hickory-nuts, dried sweet corn, he at first passed by, and peanuts I could not tempt him to touch at all. He was at first indifferent to the rice, but, on nibbling at it and finding it toothsome, he began to fill his pockets with it. Amid the rice I scattered puffed wheat. This he repeatedly took up and chipped into, at-tracted probably to the odor, but, finding it hollow, or at least very spongy and unsubstantial in its interior, he quickly dropped it. It was not solid enough to get into his winter stores

From previous experience I calculated the capacity of his chamber to be not more than four or five quarts. One day I gave him all I thought he could manage—enough, I fancied, to fill his chamber full—two quarts of hickory-nuts and some corn. How he responded to the invitation! How he flew over the course from my den to his! He fairly panted. The day might prove too short for him, or some other chipmunk might discover the pile of treasures. Three, and often four, nuts at a time, went into his pockets. If one of them was too large to go in readily, he would take it between his teeth. He would first bite off the sharp point from the nut to keep it from pricking or irritating his pouches. I do not think he feared a puncture. I re-newed the pile of nuts from time to time, and looked on with interest. The day was cloudy and wet, but he ran his express train all day. His feet soon became muddy, and it was amusing to see him wash his face with those soiled paws every time he emerged from his hole. It was striking to see how much like a machine he behaved, going through the same motions at the same points, as regularly as a clock.

As the day declined, and the pile of nuts was ever renewed, I thought I saw signs that he was either getting discouraged or else that his den was getting too full. But my inference was wrong. The next day he was back again, carrying away a fresh supply of nuts as eagerly as before. Two more quarts disappeared before night.

My enforced absence for a few days prevented me from witnessing all that happened, but a friend took notes for me. He tried to fool the chipmunk with a light-colored marble placed among the nuts. The chipmunk picked it up, but quickly dropped it. Watching his opportunity, my friend rubbed the marble with the meat of a hickory-nut. The chipmunk smelled it; then put it in his pocket; then took it out, held it in his paws a moment and looked at it, and returned it to his pocket. Three times he did this before rejecting it. Evidently his sense of taste discredited his sense of smell.

On my return at the end of the week, the enthusiasm of the chipmunk had greatly abated. He was seldom out of his den. A nut or two placed at its entrance disappeared, but he visited me no more in my study. Other chipmunks were active on all sides, but his solicitude about the winter had passed, or rather his hoarding instinct had been sated. His cellar was full. The rumor that right here was a land of plenty seemed to have gone abroad upon the air, and other chipmunks appeared upon the scene. Red squirrels and gray squirrels came, but we wasted no nuts upon them.

A female chipmunk that came and occupied an old den at my doorstep was encouraged, however. She soon became as familiar as my first acquaintance, climbing to my table,

taking nuts from my hand, and nipping my fingers spite-
fully when I held on to the nuts. Her behavior was as
nearly like that of the other as two peas are alike. I gave her
a fair supply of winter stores, but did not put her greed to
the test.

A chipmunk

So far as I have observed, the two sexes do not winter
together, and there seems to be no sort of *camaraderie*
between them. One day, earlier in this history, I saw my
male neighbor chase a smaller chipmunk, which I have
little doubt was this female, out of the study and off into
the stone wall, with great spitefulness. All-the-year-round
love among the wild creatures is very rare, if it occurs at
all. Love is seasonal and brief among most of them. My
little recluse has ample supplies for quite a family, but I
am certain he will spend the winter alone there in the
darkness of his subterranean dwelling. He must have at
least a peck of nuts that we gave him, besides all the sup-

plies that he carried in from his foraging about the orchard and the fields earlier in the season. The temptation to dig down and uncover his treasures is very great, but my curiosity might lead to his undoing, at least to his serious discomfort, so I shall forbear, resting content in the thought that at least one fellow mortal has got all that his heart desires.

As our lives have touched here at my writing-table, each working out his life-problems, I have thought of what a gulf divides my little friend and me; yet he is as earnestly solving his problems as I am mine; though, of course, he does not worry over them, or take thought of them, as I do. I cannot even say that something not himself takes thought for him; there is no thought in the matter; there is what we have to call impulse, instinct, inherited habit, and the like, though these are only terms for mysteries. He, too, shares in this wonderful something we call life. The evolutionary struggle and unfolding was for him as well as for me. He, too, is a tiny bubble on the vast current of animate nature, whose beginning is beyond our ken in the dim past, and whose ending is equally beyond our ken in the dim future.

He goes his pretty ways, gathers his precarious harvest, has his adventures, his hairbreadth escapes, his summer activity, his autumn plenty, his winter solitude and gloom, and his spring awakening and gladness. He has made himself a home here in the old orchard; he knows how deep to go into the ground to get beyond the frost-line; he is a pensioner upon the great bounty upon which we all draw, and probably lives up to the standard of the chipmunk life more nearly than most of us live up to the best standards of human life. May he so continue to live, and may we yet meet for many summers under the appleboughs.

2

Camping with President Roosevelt

[When Theodore Roosevelt as President of the United
States went to Wyoming to see the Yellowstone, he in-
vited his friend John Burroughs to accompany him. They
shared an interest in birds and out-of-door life. The following is from a book John Burroughs wrote about this
trip and his impressions of the President.

They left Washington by train on April 1 and though
it was already spring in the Capital, they encountered ice
and snow before their journey ended. When they reached
Gardiner, the entrance to the Park, John Burroughs's first
experience was a hair-raising one, for the mules drawing
his conveyance set off at such a lively pace that he had to
grip the seat with both hands.]

"Well," I said to myself, "they are giving me a regular
Western send-off;" and I thought, as the conveyance swayed
from side to side, that it would suit me just as well if my
driver did not try to keep up with the presidential procession. The driver and his mules were shut off from me by a
curtain, but, looking ahead out of the sides of the ve-
hicle, I saw two good-sized logs lying across our course.
Surely, I thought (and barely had time to think) , he will
avoid these. But he did not, and as we passed over them

Teddy Roosevelt at Yellowstone

I was nearly thrown through the top of the carriage. "This *is* a lively send-off," I said rubbing my bruises with one hand, while I clung to the seat with the other. Presently I saw the cowboys scrambling up the bank as if to get out of our way: then the President on his fine gray stallion scrambling up the bank with his escort, and looking ominously in my direction, as we thundered by.

"Well," I said, "This is indeed a novel ride; for once in my life I have side-tracked the President of the United States! I am given the right of way over all." On we tore, along the smooth, hard road, and did not slacken our pace till, at the end of a mile or two, we began to mount the hill toward Fort Yellowstone. And not till we reached the fort did I learn that our mules had run away. They had been excited beyond control by the presidential cavalcade, and the driver, finding he could not hold them, had aimed only to keep them in the road, and we very soon had the road all to ourselves.

[Later when the party proceeded to a camp in the gorge of the Yellowstone River, the naturalist was given a horse to ride.]

About two miles from camp we came to a picket of two or three soldiers, where my big bay was waiting for me and I mounted him. Except for an hour's riding the day before, I had not been on a horse's back for nearly fifty years. The first sense of a live, spirited, powerful animal beneath you, at whose mercy you are—you, a pedestrian all your days—with gullies and rocks and logs to cross, and deep chasms opening close beside you, is not a little disturbing. But my big bay did his part well, and I did not lose my head or my nerve, as we cautiously made our way along the narrow path on the side of the steep gorge, with a foaming torrent rushing along at its foot, nor yet when we forded the rocky and rapid Yellowstone. A misstep or a stumble on the part of my steed, and probably the first bubble of my confidence would have been shivered at once; but this did not happen, and in due time we reached the group of tents that formed the President's camp.

While in camp we always had a big fire at night in the open near the tents, and around this we sat upon logs or camp-stools, and listened to the President's talk. What a stream of it he poured forth! and what a varied and picturesque stream!—anecdote, history, science, politics, adventure, literature; bits of his experience as a ranchman, hunter, Rough Rider, legislator, civil service commissioner, police commissioner, governor, president—the frankest confessions, the most telling criticisms, happy characterizations of prominent political leaders, or foreign rulers, or members of his own Cabinet; always surprising by his candor, astonishing by his memory, and diverting by his humor. His reading has been very wide, and he has that rare type of memory which retains details as well as mass and generalities. One night something started him off on ancient history, and one would have thought he was just fresh from his college course in history, the dates and names and events came so readily.

We went up into the geyser region with sleighs, each drawn by four horses. A big snowbank had to be shoveled through for us before we got to the Golden Gate, two miles above Mammoth Hot Springs. Beyond that we were at an altitude of about eight thousand feet, on a fairly level course that led now through woods, and now through open country, with the snow of a uniform depth of four or five feet, except as we neared the "formations," where the subterranean warmth kept the ground bare. The roads had been broken and the snow packed for us by teams from the fort, otherwise the journey would have been impossible.

As one nears the geyser region, he gets the impression from the columns of steam going up here and there in the distance—now from behind a piece of woods, now from out a hidden valley—that he is approaching a manufacturing center, or a railroad terminus. And when he begins to hear the hoarse snoring of "Roaring Mountain," the illusion is still more complete. At Norris's there is a big vent where the stream comes tearing out of a recent hole in the ground with terrific force. Huge mounds of ice had formed from the congealed vapor all around it, some of them very striking.

At Norris's the hotel room that the President and I occupied was on the ground floor, and was heated by a huge box stove. As we entered it to go to bed, the President said, "Oom John, don't you think it is too hot here?" [Oom is the Dutch word for uncle; it is also a term of affection.]

"I certainly do," I replied.

"Shall I open the window?"

"That will just suit me." And he threw the sash, which came down to the floor, all the way up, making an opening like a doorway. The night was cold, but neither of us suffered from the abundance of fresh air.

The caretaker of the building was a big Swede called Andy. In the morning Andy said that beat him: "There was the President of the United States sleeping in that room, with the window open to the floor, and not so much as one soldier outside on guard."

One afternoon at Norris's, the President and I took a walk to observe the birds. In the grove about the barns there was a great number, the most attractive to me being the mountain bluebird. These birds we saw in all parts of the Park, and at Norris's there was an unusual number of them. How blue they were—breast and all! In voice and manner they were almost identical with our bluebird. The Western purple finch was abundant here also, and juncos, and several kinds of sparrows, with an occasional Western robin.

Throughout the trip I found his interest in bird life very keen, and his eye and ear remarkably quick. He usually saw the bird or heard its note as quickly as I did—and I had nothing else to think about, and had been teaching my eye and ear the trick of it for over fifty years. Of course, his training as a big game hunter stood him in good stead, but back of that were his naturalist's instincts, and his genuine love of all forms of wild life.

The President had counted much on seeing the bears that in summer board at the Fountain Hotel, but they were not yet out of their dens. We saw the track of only one, and he was not making for the hotel. At all the formations where the geysers are, the ground was bare over a large area. I even saw a wild flower—an early buttercup, not an inch high—in bloom. This seems to be the earliest wild flower in the Rockies. It is the only fragrant buttercup I know.

As we were riding along in our big sleigh toward the Fountain Hotel, the President suddenly jumped out, and, with his soft hat as a shield to his hand, captured a mouse that was running along over the ground near us. He wanted it for Dr. Merriam, on the chance that it might be a new species. While we all went fishing in the afternoon, the President skinned his mouse, and prepared the pelt to be sent to Washington. It was done as neatly as a professed taxidermist would have done it. This was the only game the President killed in the Park. In relating the incident to a reporter while I was in Spokane, the thought occurred to me, Suppose he changes that *u* to an *o,* and makes the President capture a moose, what a pickle I shall be in! Is it anything more than an ordinary newspaper enterprise to turn a mouse into a moose? But, luckily for me, no such metamorphosis happened to that little mouse. It turned out not to be a new species as it should have been, but a species new to the Park.

At the Cañon Hotel the snow was very deep, and had become so soft from the warmth of the earth beneath, as well as from the sun above, that we could only reach the brink of the Cañon on skis. The President and Major Pitcher had used skis before, but I had not, and, starting out without the customary pole, I soon came to grief. The snow gave way beneath me, and I was soon in an awkward predicament. The more I struggled, the lower my head and shoulders went, till only my heels, strapped to those long timbers, protruded above the snow. To reverse my position was impossible till some one came and reached me the end of a pole, and pulled me upright. But I very soon got the hang of the things, and the President and I quickly left the superintendent behind. I think I could have passed the President, but my manners forbade. He was heavier than I was, and broke in more. When one of his feet would go down half a yard or more, I noted with admiration the skilled diplomacy he displayed in extricating it. The tendency of my skis was all the time to diverge, and each to go off at an acute angle to my main course, and I had constantly to be on the alert to check this tendency.

In front of the hotel were some low hills separated by gentle valleys. At the President's suggestion, he and I raced on our skis down those inclines. We had only to stand up straight, and let gravity do the rest. As we were going swiftly down the side of one of the hills, I saw out of the corner of my eye the President taking a header into the snow. The snow had given way beneath him, and nothing could save him from taking the plunge. I don't know whether I called out, or only thought, something about the downfall of the administration. At any rate, the administration was down, and pretty well buried, but it was quickly on its feet again, shaking the snow with a boy's laughter. I kept straight on, and very soon the laugh was on me, for the treacherous snow sank beneath me, and I took a header, too.

"Who is laughing now, Oom John?" called out the President.

The spirit of the boy was in the air that day about the Cañon of the Yellowstone, and the biggest boy of us all was President Roosevelt.

The snow was getting so soft in the middle of the day that our return to the Mammoth Hot Springs could no longer be delayed. Accordingly, we were up in the morning, and ready to start on the home journey, a distance of twenty miles, by four o'clock. The snow bore up the horses well till mid-forenoon, when it began to give way beneath them. But by very careful management we pulled through without serious delay, and were back again at the house of Major Pitcher in time for luncheon, being the only outsiders who had ever made the tour of the Park so early in the season.

A few days later I bade good-by to the President, who went on his way to California, while I made a loop of travel to Spokane, and around through Idaho and Montana, and had glimpses of the great, optimistic, sunshiny West that I shall not soon forget.

3

Migrating Birds and Bird-Songs

One of the new pleasures of country life when one has made the acquaintance of the birds is to witness the northward bird procession as it passes or tarries with us in the spring—a procession which lasts from April till June and has some new feature daily.

That birds have a sense of home and return in most cases to their old haunts, is quite certain. A friend of mine has a summer home in one of the more secluded valleys of the Catskills, and every June for three years a pair of catbirds have nested near the house; and every day, many times, one or both birds come to the dining-room window, for sweet butter. Very soon after their arrival they appear at the window, shy at first, but soon becoming so tame that they approach within a few feet of the mistress of the house. They light on the chairbacks and sometimes even hop on the table, taking the butter from the fork she holds for them. Their behavior now is very convincing that one or both have been at the window for butter in previous years.

One sees the passing bird procession in his own grounds and neighborhood without pausing to think that in every man's grounds and in every neighborhood throughout the

State, and throughout a long broad belt of States, about several millions of homes, and over several millions of farms, the same flood-tide of bird-life is creeping and eddying or sweeping over the land. It is moving day on a continental scale. It is the call of the primal instinct to increase and multiply, suddenly setting in motion whole tribes and races. The first phoebe-bird, the first song sparrow, the first robin or bluebird in March or early April, is like the first ripple of the rising tide on the shore.

Think of the myriads of dooryards where the "chippies" are just arriving; of the blooming orchards where the pass-

Warbler in the blossoms

ing many-colored warblers are eagerly inspecting the buds
and leaves; of the woods and woody streams where the
oven-birds and water-thrushes are searching out their old
haunts; of the secluded bushy fields and tangles where
the chewinks, the brown thrashers, the chats, the catbirds,
are once more preparing to begin life anew—think of all
this and more, and you may get some idea of the extent
and importance of our bird-life.

I fancy that on almost any day in mid-May the flickers
are drilling their holes into a million or more decayed
trees between the Hudson and the Mississippi; that any
day a month earlier the phoebes are starting their nests
under a million or more woodsheds or bridges or overhanging rocks; that several millions of robins are carrying mud and straws to sheltered projections about buildings, or to the big forked branches in the orchards.

Considering the enormous number of birds of all species
that flood the continent at this season, as if some dike or
barrier south of us had suddenly given way, one wonders
where they could all have been pent up during the winter.
Mexico and Central and South America have their own
bird populations the seasons through; and with the addi-
tion of the hosts from this country, it seems as if those
lands must have literally swarmed with birds, and that the
food question (as with us) must have been pressing. Of
course, a great many of our birds—such as sparrows, robins,
blackbirds, meadowlarks, jays, and chewinks—spend the
winter in the Southern States, but many more—warblers,
swallows, swifts, hummers, orioles, tanagers, cuckoos, fly-
catchers, vireos, and others—seek out the equatorial region.

The waves of bird migrants roll on through the States
into Canada and beyond, breaking like waves on the shore,
and spreading their contents over large areas. The warbler
wave spends itself largely in the forests and mountains
of the northern tier of States and Canada, its utmost range
reaching beyond the Artic Circle, while its content of

ground warblers, such as the Maryland yellow-throat, begins to drop out south of the Potomac and in Ohio. The robins cover a very wide area, as do the song sparrows, the kingbirds, the vireos, the flickers, the orioles, the catbirds, and others.

As the birds begin to arrive from the South in the spring, the birds that have come down from the North to spend the winter with us—the crossbills, the pine grosbeaks, the pine linnets, the red-breasted nuthatches, the juncos, and the snow buntings—begin to withdraw. The ebb of one species follows the flow of another. One winter, in December, a solitary red-breasted nuthatch took up his abode with me, attracted by the suet and nuts I had placed on a maple-tree-trunk in front of my study window for the downy woodpecker, the chickadees, and the native nuthatches. Red-breasted evidently said to himself, "Needless to look farther."

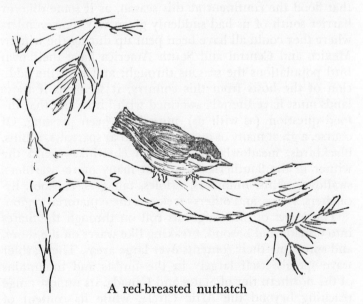

A red-breasted nuthatch

He took lodgings in a wren-box on a post near by, and at night and during windy, stormy days was securely housed there. He tarried till April, and his constancy, his pretty form, and his engaging ways greatly endeared him to us. The pair of white-breasted nuthatches that fed at the same table looked coarse and common beside this little delicate waif from the far North. He could not stand to see lying about a superabundance of cracked hickory-nuts, any more than his larger relatives could, and would work industriously carrying them away and hiding them in the woodpile and summer-house near by. The other nuthatches bossed him, as they in turn were bossed by Downy, and as he in turn bossed the brown creeper and the chickadees. In early April my little red-breast disappeared, and I fancied him turning his face northward, urged by a stronger impulse than that for food and shelter merely. He was my tiny guest from unknown lands, my baby bird, and he left a vacancy that none of the others could fill.

Some birds passing north in the spring are provokingly silent. Every April I see the hermit thrush hopping about the woods, and in case of a sudden snowstorm seeking shelter about the out-buildings; but I never hear even a fragment of his wild, silvery strain. The white-crowned sparrow also passes in silence. I see the bird for a few days about the same date each year, but he will not reveal to me his song. On the other hand, his congener, the white-throated sparrow, is decidedly musical in passing, both spring and fall. His sweet, wavering whistle is at times quite as full and perfect as when heard in June or July in the Canadian woods. The latter bird is much more numerous than the white-crowned, and its stay with us more protracted, which may in a measure account for the greater frequency of its song. The fox sparrow, who passes earlier (sometimes in March), is also chary of the music with which he is so richly endowed. It is not every season that I hear him, though my ear is on the alert for his strong, finely-modulated whistle.

Nearly all the warblers sing in passing. I hear them in the orchards, in the groves, in the woods, as they pause to feed in their northward journey, their brief, lisping, shuffling, insect-like notes requiring to be searched for by the ear, as their forms by the eye. But the ear is not tasked to identify the songs of the kinglets, as they tarry briefly with us in spring. In fact, there is generally a week in April or early May, during which the piping, voluble, rapid, intricate, and delicious warble of the ruby-crowned kinglet is the most noticeable strain to be heard, especially among the evergreens.

The songless birds—why has Nature denied them this gift? But they nearly all have some musical call or impulse that serves them very well. The quail has his whistle, the woodpecker his drum, the pewee his plaintive cry, the chickadee his exquisitely sweet call, the highhole his long, repeated "wick, wick, wick," one of the most welcome sounds of spring, the jay his musical gurgle, the hawk his scream, the crow his sturdy caw. Only one of our pretty birds of the orchard is reduced to an all but inaudible note, and that is the cedar-bird.

It is not generally known that individual birds of the same species show different degrees of musical ability. This is often noticed in caged birds, among which the principle of variation seems more active; but an attentive observer notes the same fact in wild birds. Occasionally he hears one that in powers of song surpasses all its fellows. I have heard a sparrow, an oriole, and a wood thrush, each of which had a song of its own that far exceeded any other. I stood one day by a trout-stream, and suspended my fishing for several minutes to watch a song sparrow that was singing on a dry limb before me. He had five distinct songs, each as markedly different from the others as any human songs, which he repeated one after the other. He may have had a sixth or a seventh, but he bethought himself of some business in the next field, and flew away before he had exhausted his repertory.

I once had a letter from Robert Louis Stevenson, who said he had read an account I had written of the song of the English blackbird. He said I might as well talk of the song of man; that every blackbird had its own song; and then he told me of a remarkable singer he used to hear somewhere amid the Scottish hills. But his singer was, of course, an exception: twenty-four blackbirds out of every twenty-five probably sing the same song, with no appreciable variations: but the twenty-fifth may show extraordinary powers.

I told Stevenson that his famous singer had probably been to school to some nightingale on the Continent or in southern England. I might have told him of the robin I once heard here that sang with great spirit and accuracy the song of the brown thrasher, or of another that had the note of the whip-poor-will interpolated in the regular robin song, or of still another that had the call of the quail. In each case the bird had probably heard the song and learned it while very young. In the Trossachs, in Scotland, I followed a song thrush about for a long time, attracted by its peculiar song. It repeated over and over again three or four notes of a well-known air, which it might have caught from some shepherd boy whistling to his flock or to his cow.

The power of bird-songs over us is so much a matter of association that every traveler to other countries finds the feathered songsters of less merit than those he left behind. The stranger does not hear the birds in the same receptive, uncritical frame of mind as does the native; they are not in the same way the voices of the place and the season. What music can there be in that long, piercing far-heard note of the first meadowlark in spring to any but a native, or in the "o-ka-lee" of the red-winged blackbird as he rests upon the willows in March?

If we have no associations with these sounds, they will mean very little to us. I am always disturbed when persons not especially observant of birds ask me to take them where they can hear a particular bird, in whose song they have become interested through a description in some book. As I listen with them, I feel like apologizing for the bird: it has a bad cold, or has just heard some depressing news; it will not let itself out. The song seems so casual and minor when you make a dead set at it. I have taken persons to hear the hermit thrush, and I have fancied that they were all the time saying to themselves, "Is that all?" But should one hear the bird in his walk, when the mind is attuned to simple things and is open and receptive, when expectation is not aroused and the song comes as a surprise out of the dusky silence of the woods, then one feels that it merits all the fine things that can be said of it.

Bird-songs are not music, properly speaking, but only suggestions of music. It is as signs of joy and love in nature, as heralds of spring, and as the spirit of the woods and fields made audible, that they appeal to us.

4

The Pastoral Bees

[One of the objects of his walks was to look for hollow trees where wild bees were producing honey. His interest in bees led him to have his own beehives at Riverby.]

The honey-bee goes forth from the hive in spring like the dove from Noah's ark, and it is not till after many days that she brings back the olive leaf, which in this case is a pellet of golden pollen upon each hip, usually obtained from the alder or swamp willow. In a country where maple sugar is made, the bees get their first taste of sweet from the sap as it flows from the spiles, or as it dries and is condensed upon the sides of the buckets. They will sometimes, in their eagerness, come about the boiling place and be overwhelmed by the steam and the smoke. But bees appear to be more eager for bread in the spring than for honey; their supply of this article, perhaps, does not keep as well as their stores of the latter; hence fresh bread, in the shape of new pollen, is diligently sought for.

My bees get their first supplies from the catkins of the willows. How quickly they find them out. If but one catkin opens anywhere within range, a bee is on hand that very hour to rifle it, and it is a most pleasing experience to stand near the hive some mild April day and see

A bee and a linden

them come pouring in with their little baskets packed with this first fruitage of the spring. They will have new bread now; they have been to mill in good earnest; see their dusty coats, and the golden grist they bring home with them.

When a bee brings pollen into the hive, he advances to the cell in which it is to be deposited and kicks it off as one might his overalls or rubber boots, making one foot help the other; then he walks off without ever looking behind him; another bee, one of the indoor hands, comes along and rams it down with his head and packs it into the cell as the dairy-maid packs butter into a firkin.

The first honey is perhaps obtained from the flowers of the red maple and the golden willow. The latter sends forth a wild, delicious perfume. The sugar maple blooms a little later, and from its silken tassels a rich nectar is gathered. Yet evidently it is not the perfume of any flower that attracts the bees; they pay no attention to the sweet-scented lilac, or to heliotrope, but work upon sumac, silkweed, and the hateful snapdragon.

It is the making of the wax that costs with the bee. The honey he can have for the gathering, but the wax he must make himself. When wax is to be made the wax-makers fill themselves with honey and retire into their chamber for private meditation; it is like some solemn religious rite; they take hold of hands, or hook themselves together in long lines that hang in festoons from the top of the hive, and wait for the miracle to transpire. After about twenty-four hours their patience is rewarded, the honey is turned into wax, minute scales of which are secreted from between the rings of the abdomen of each bee; this is taken off and from it the comb is built up. It is calculated that about twenty-five pounds of honey are used in elaborating one pound of comb, to say nothing of the time that is lost. Hence the importance, in an economical point of view, of a recent device by which the honey is extracted and the comb returned to the bees.

The drones have the least enviable time of it: their foothold in the hive is very precarious. They look like the giants, the lords of the swarm, but they are really the tools. Their loud threatening hum has no sting to back it up, and their size and noise make them only the more conspicuous marks for the birds.

Toward the close of the season, say in July or August, the fiat goes forth that the drones must die; there is no further use for them. Then the poor creatures, how they are huddled and hustled about, trying to hide in corners and by-ways. There is no loud, defiant humming now, but abject fear seizes them. They cower like hunted criminals. I have seen a dozen or more of them wedge themselves into a small space between the glass and the comb, where the bees could not get hold of them, or where they seemed to be overlooked in the general slaughter. They will also crawl outside and hide under the edges of the hive. But sooner or later they are all killed or kicked out. The drone makes no resistance, except to pull back and try to get away; but (putting yourself in his place) with one bee a-hold of your collar or the hair of your head, and another a-hold of each arm or leg, and still another feeling for your waistbands with his sting, the odds are greatly against you.

It is a singular fact, also, that the queen is made, not born. If the entire population of Spain or Great Britain were the offspring of one mother, it might be found necesstry to hit upon some device by which a royal baby could be manufactured out of an ordinary one, or else give up the fashion of royalty. All the bees in the hive have a common parentage, and the queen and the worker are the same in the egg and in the chick; the patent of royalty is in the cell and in the food; the cell being much larger, and the food a peculiar stimulating kind of jelly. In certain contingencies, such as the loss of the queen with no eggs in the royal cells, the workers take the larva of an ordinary bee, enlarge the cell by taking in the two adjoining ones, and nurse it and stuff it and coddle it, till at the end of sixteen days it comes out a queen. But ordinarily, in the natural course of events, the young queen is kept a prisoner in her cell till the old queen has left with the swarm.

I always feel that I have missed some good fortune if I am away from home when my bees swarm. What a delightful summer sound it is! How they come pouring out of the hive, twenty or thirty thousand bees, each striving to get out first! It is as when the dam gives way and lets the waters loose; it is a flood of bees which breaks upward into the air, and becomes a maze of whirling black lines to the eye, and a soft chorus of myriad musical sounds to the ear. That every new swarm contemplates migrating to the woods, seems confirmed by the fact that they will only come out when the weather is favorable to such an enterprise. For all bees are wild bees and incapable of domestication; that is, the instinct to go back to nature and take up again their wild abodes in the trees is never eradicated.

When a swarm migrates to the woods, the individual bees, as I have intimated, do not move in right lines or straight forward, like a flock of birds, but round and round, like chaff in a whirlwind. This way and that way they drift, now contracting, now expanding, rising, sinking, growing thick about some branch or bush, then dispersing and massing at some other point, till finally they begin to alight in earnest, when in a few moments the whole swarm is collected upon the branch, forming a bunch perhaps as large as a two-gallon measure. Here they will hang from one to three or four hours or until a suitable tree in the woods is looked up, when, if they have not been offered a hive in the meantime, they are up and off.

As they take a direct course, there is always some chance of following them to the tree. If the bees are successfully followed to their retreat, two plans are feasible—either to fell the tree at once, and seek to hive them, perhaps bring them home in the section of the tree that contains the cavity; or to leave the tree until fall, then invite your neighbors and go and cut it, and see the ground flow with honey. The former course is more business-like; but the latter is the one usually recommended by one's friends and neighbors.

The notion has always very generally prevailed that the queen of the bees is an absolute ruler, and issues her royal orders to willing subjects. Hence Napoleon the First sprinkled the symbolic bees over the imperial mantle that bore the arms of his dynasty; and in the country of the Pharaohs the bee was used as the emblem of a people submissive to the orders of its king. But the fact is, a swarm of bees is an absolute democracy, and kings and despots can find no warrant in their example. The power

and authority are entirely vested in the great mass, the
workers. They furnish all the brains and foresight of the
colony, and administer its affairs. Their word is law, and
both king and queen must obey. They regulate the swarm-
ing, and give the signal for the swarm to issue from the
hive; they select and make ready the tree in the woods
and conduct the queen to it.

The peculiar office and sacredness of the queen consists
in the fact that she is the mother of the swarm, and the
bees love and cherish her as a mother and not as a sover-
eign. She is the sole female bee in the hive, and the swarm
clings to her because she is their life. Deprived of their
queen, and of all brood from which to rear one, the swarm
loses all heart and soon dies, though there be an abundance
of honey in the hive.

The common bees will never use their sting upon the
queen; if she is to be disposed of they starve her to death;
and the queen herself will sting nothing but royalty—
nothing but a rival queen.

The queen, I say, is the mother bee; it is undoubtedly
complimenting her to call her a queen and invest her with
regal authority, yet she is a superb creature, and looks
every inch a queen. It is an event to distinguish her amid
the mass of bees when the swarm alights; it awakens a
thrill. Before you have seen a queen you wonder if this or
that bee, which seems a little larger than its fellows, is not
she, but when you once really set eyes upon her you do
not doubt for a moment. You know *that* is the queen.
That long, elegant, shining, feminine-looking creature
can be none less than royalty. How beautifully her body
tapers, how distinguished she looks, how deliberate her
movements! The bees do not fall down before her, but
caress her and touch her person. The drones or males, are
large bees too, but coarse, blunt, broad-shouldered, mas-
culine-looking.

The life of a swarm of bees is like an active and hazardous campaign of an army; the ranks are being continually depleted, and continually recruited. What adventures they have by flood and field, and what hair-breadth escapes! A strong swarm during the honey season loses, on an average, about four or five thousand per month, or one hundred and fifty per day. They are overwhelmed by wind and rain, caught by spiders, benumbed by cold, crushed by cattle, drowned in rivers and ponds, and in many nameless ways cut off or disabled.

In the spring the principal mortality is from the cold. As the sun declines they get chilled before they can reach home. Many fall down outside the hive, unable to get in with their burden. One may see them come utterly spent and drop hopelessly into the grass in front of their very doors. Before they can rest the cold has stiffened them. I go out in April and May and pick them up by the handfuls, their baskets loaded with pollen, and warm them in the sun or in the house, or by the simple warmth of my hand, until they can crawl into the hive. Heat is their life, and an apparently lifeless bee may be revived by warming him. I have also picked them up while rowing on the river and seen them safely to shore. It is amusing to see them come hurrying home when there is a thunderstorm approaching. They come piling in till the rain is upon them. Those that are overtaken by the storm doubtless weather it as best they can in the sheltering trees or grass.

It is not probable that a bee ever gets lost by wandering into strange and unknown parts. With their myriad eyes they see everything; and then, their sense of locality is very acute, is, indeed, one of their ruling traits. When a bee marks the place of his hive, or of a bit of good pasturage in the fields or swamps, or of the bee-hunter's box of honey on the hills or in the woods, he returns to it as unerringly as fate.

5

A Young Marsh Hawk

Most country boys, I fancy, know the marsh hawk. It is he
you see flying low over the fields, beating about bushes
and marshes and dipping over the fences, with his attention directed to the ground beneath him. He is a cat on
wings. He keeps so low that the birds and mice do not see
him till he is fairly upon them. The hen-hawk swoops
down upon the meadow-mouse from his position high in
air, or from the top of a dead tree; but the marsh hawk
stalks him and comes suddenly upon him from over the
fence, or from behind a low bush or tuft of grass. He is
nearly as large as the hen-hawk, but has a much longer
tail. When I was a boy I used to call him the long-tailed
hawk. The male is a bluish slate color; the female a reddish
brown, like the hen-hawk, with a white rump.

Unlike the other hawks, they nest on the ground in low,
thick marshy places. For several seasons a pair have nested
in a bushy marsh a few miles back of me, near the house
of a farmer friend of mine, who has a keen eye for the wild
life about him. Two years ago he found the nest, but when
I got over to see it the next week, it had been robbed,
probably by some boys in the neighborhood.

The past season, in April or May, by watching the

54

Hawk on her nest

mother bird, he found the nest again. It was in a marshy place, several acres in extent, in the bottom of a valley, and thickly grown with hardhack, prickly ash, smilax, and other low thorny bushes. My friend brought me to the brink of a low hill, and pointed out to me in the marsh below us, as nearly as he could, just where the nest was located. Then we crossed the pasture, entered upon the marsh, and made our way cautiously toward it. The wild thorny growths, waist high, had to be carefully dealt with.

As we neared the spot I used my eyes the best I could, but I did not see the hawk till she sprang into the air not ten yards away from us. She went screaming upward, and was soon sailing in a circle far above us. There, on a coarse matting of twigs and weeds, lay five snow-white eggs, a little more than half as large as hens' eggs. My companion said the male hawk would probably soon appear and join the female, but he did not. She kept drifting away to the east, and was soon gone from our sight.

In about a week I paid another visit to the hawk's nest. The eggs were all hatched, and the mother bird was hovering near. I shall never forget the curious expression of those young hawks sitting there on the ground. The expression was not one of youth, but of extreme age. Such an ancient, infirm look as they had—the sharp, dark, and shrunken look about the face and eyes, and their feeble, tottering motions! They sat upon their elbows and the hind part of their bodies, and their pale, withered legs and feet extended before them in the most helpless fashion. Their angular bodies were covered with a pale yellowish down, like that of a chicken; their heads had a plucked, seedy appearance; and their long, strong, naked wings hung down by their sides till they touched the ground: power and ferocity in the first rude draught, shorn of everything but its sinister ugliness. Another curious thing was the gradation of the young in size; they tapered down regularly from the first to the fifth, as if there had been, as probably there was, an interval of a day or two between the hatching of each.

The two older ones showed some signs of fear on our approach, and one of them threw himself upon his back, and put up his impotent legs, and glared at us with open beak. The two smaller ones regarded us not at all. Neither of the parent birds appeared during our stay.

When I visited the nest again, eight or ten days later, the birds were much grown, but of as marked a difference in size as before, and with the same look of extreme old age,—old age in men of the aquiline type, nose and chin coming together, and eyes large and sunken. They now glared upon us with a wild, savage look, and opened their beaks threateningly.

The next week, when my friend visited the nest, the larger of the hawks fought him savagely. But one of the brood, probably the last to hatch, had made but little growth. It appeared to be on the point of starvation. Did the larger and stronger young devour all the food before the weaker member could obtain any? Probably this was the case.

My friend brought the feeble nestling away, and the same day my little boy got it and brought it home, wrapped in a woolen rag. It was clearly a starved bantling. It cried feebly, but would not lift up its head.

We first poured some warm milk down its throat, which soon revived it, so that it would swallow small bits of flesh. In a day or two we had it eating ravenously, and its growth became noticeable. Its voice had the sharp whistling character of that of its parents, and was stilled only when the bird was asleep. We made a pen for it, about a yard square, in one end of the study, covering the floor with several thicknesses of newspapers; and here, upon a bit of brown woolen blanket for a nest, the hawk waxed strong day by day. An uglier-looking pet, tested by all the rules we usually apply to such things, would have been hard to find. There he would sit upon his elbows, his helpless feet out in front of him, his great featherless wings touching the floor, and shrilly cry for more food. For a time we gave him water daily from a stylograph-pen filler, but the water he evidently did not need or relish. Fresh meat, and plenty of it, was his demand. And we soon discovered that he liked game, such as mice, squirrels, birds, much better than butcher's meat.

Then began a lively campaign on the part of my little boy against all the vermin and small game in the neighborhood to keep the hawk supplied. He trapped and he hunted, he enlisted his mates in his service, he even robbed the cats to feed the hawk. "Where is Julian?" "Gone after a squirrel for his hawk." And often the day would be half gone before his hunt was successful. The premises were very soon cleared of mice, and the vicinity of chipmunks and squirrels. Farther and farther he was compelled to hunt the surrounding farms and woods to keep up with the demands of the hawk.

The hawk's plumage very soon began to show itself, crowding off tufts of the down. The quills on his great wings sprouted and grew apace. What a ragged, uncanny appearance he presented! But his look of extreme age gradually became modified. His legs developed nearly as slowly as his wings. He could not stand steadily upon them till about ten days before he was ready to fly. The talons were limp and feeble. When we came with food he would hobble along toward us like the worst kind of a cripple, dropping and moving his wings, and treading upon his legs from the foot back to the elbow, the foot remaining closed and useless. Like a baby learning to stand, he made many trials before he succeeded. He would rise up on his trembling legs only to fall back again.

One day, in the summer-house, I saw him for the first time stand for a moment squarely upon his legs with the feet fully spread beneath them. He looked about him as if the world suddenly wore a new aspect.

It was now the 20th of July, and the hawk was about five weeks old. In a day or two he was walking or jumping about the ground. He chose a position under the edge of a Norway spruce, where he would sit for hours dozing, or looking out upon the landscape. When we brought him game he would advance to meet us with wings slightly lifted, and uttering a shrill cry. Toss him a mouse and he would seize it with one foot and hop off to his cover, where he would bend above it, spread his plumage, look this way and that, uttering all the time the most exultant and satisfied chuckle.

About this time he began to practice striking with his talons, as an Indian boy might begin practicing with his bow and arrow. He would strike at a dry leaf in the grass, or at a fallen apple, or at some imaginary object. He was learning the use of his weapons. His wings also,—he seemed to feel them sprouting from his shoulder. He would lift them straight up and hold them expanded, and they would seem to quiver with excitement. Every hour in the day he would do this. The pressure was beginning to center there. Then he would strike playfully at a leaf or a bit of wood, and keep his wings lifted.

Hawk and a mouse

The next step was to spring into the air and beat his wings. He seemed now to be thinking entirely of his wings. They itched to be put to use.

A day or two later he would leap and fly several feet. A pile of brush ten or twelve feet below the bank was easily reached. Here he would perch in true hawk fashion, to the bewilderment and scandal of all the robins and cat-birds in the vicinity. Here he would dart his eye in all directions, turning his head over and glancing it up into the sky.

He was now a lovely creature, fully fledged, and as tame as a kitten. But he was not a bit like a kitten in one respect,—he could not bear to have you stroke or even touch his plumage. He had a horror of your hand, as if it would hopelessly defile him. But he would perch upon it, and allow you to carry him about. If a dog or cat appeared, he was ready to give battle instantly. He rushed up to a little dog one day, and struck him with his foot savagely. He was afraid of strangers, and of any unusual object.

The last week in July he began to fly quite freely, and it was necessary to clip one of his wings. As the clipping embraced only the ends of his primaries, he soon overcame the difficulty, and by carrying his broad, long tail more on that side, flew with considerable ease. He made longer and longer excursions into the surrounding fields and vineyards, and did not always return. On such occasions we would go find him and fetch him back.

Late one rainy afternoon he flew away into the vineyard, and when, an hour later, I went after him, he could not be found, and we never saw him again. We hoped hunger would soon drive him back, but we have had no clew to him from that day to this.

6

Birds'-Nesting

[Today anyone seeking information about the nest of some species of bird has only to turn the pages of a bird guide to find out what he wants to know. When John Burroughs began to study birds and to write about them, bird guides did not exist. He had to make discoveries for himself. One such discovery was the nest of the black-throated blue warbler, which no one had ever described before. "Birds'-Nesting," as he called it, yielded him other pleasures as well, as he relates here.]

Birds'-Nesting is by no means a failure, even though you find no birds'-nests. You are sure to find other things of interest, plenty of them. A friend of mine says that, in his youth, he used to go hunting with his gun loaded for wild turkeys, and, though he frequently saw plenty of smaller game, he generally came home empty-handed, because he was loaded only for turkeys. But the student of ornithology, who is also a lover of Nature in all her shows and forms, does not go out loaded for turkeys merely, but for everything that moves and grows, and is quite sure, therefore, to bag some game, if not with his gun, then with his eye, or his nose, or his ear.

Even a crow's nest is not amiss, or a den in the rocks

where the coons or skunks live, or a log where a partridge
drums, or the partridge himself starting up with spread
tail, and walking a few yards in advance of you before he
goes humming through the woods, or a woodchuck hole,
with well beaten and worn entrance, and with the sap-
lings gnawed and soiled about it, or the strong, fetid smell
of the fox, which a sharp nose detects here and there, and
which is a good perfume in the woods. And then it is
enough to come upon a spring in the woods and stoop
down and drink of the sweet, cold water, and bathe your
hands in it, or to walk along a trout brook, which has
absorbed the shadows till it has itself become but a denser
shade. Then I am always drawn out of my way by a ledge
of rocks, and love nothing better than to explore the
caverns and dens, or to sit down under the overhanging
crags and let the wild scene absorb me.

There is a fascination about ledges! They are an un-
mistakable feature, and give emphasis and character to
the scene. I feel their spell, and must pause awhile. Time,
old as the hills and older, looks out of their scarred and
weather-worn face. The woods are of to-day, but the ledges,
in comparison, are of eternity. One pokes about them as
he would about ruins, and with something of the same
feeling. They are ruins of the fore world. Here the founda-
tions of the hills were laid; here the earth-giants wrought
and builded. They constrain one to silence and meditation;
the whispering and rustling trees seem trivial and impertinent.

And then there are birds'-nests about ledges, too, exquisite mossy tenements, with white, pebbly eggs, that I
can never gaze upon without emotion. The little brown
bird, the phoebe, looks at you from her niche till you are
within a few feet of her, when she darts away. Occasionally
you may find the nest of some rare wood-warbler forming
a little pocket in the apron of moss that hangs down over
the damp rocks.

The sylvan folk seem to know when you are on a peaceful mission, and are less afraid than usual. Did not that marmot to-day guess that my errand did not concern him as he saw me approach from his cover in the bushes? But when he saw me pause and deliberately seat myself on the stone wall immediately over his hole, his confidence was much shaken. He apparently deliberated awhile, for I heard the leaves rustle as if he were making up his mind, when he suddenly broke cover and came for his hole full tilt. Any other animal would have taken to his heels and fled; but a woodchuck's heels do not amount to much for speed, and he feels his only safety is in his hole. On he came in the most obstinate and determined manner, and I dare say if I had sat down in his hole, would have attacked me unhesitatingly. This I did not give him a chance to do.

But I am making slow headway toward finding the birds'-nests, for I had set out on this occasion in hopes of finding a rare nest,—the nest of the black-throated blue-backed warbler, which, it seemed, with one or two others, was still wanting to make the history of our warblers complete. The woods were extensive, and full of deep, dark tangles, and looking for any particular nest seemed about as hopeless a task as searching for a needle in a haystack, as the old saying is. Where to begin, and how? But the principle is the same as in looking for a hen's nest,—first find your bird, then watch its movements.

The bird is in these woods, for I have seen him scores of times, but whether he builds high or low, on the ground or in the trees, is all unknown to me. That is his song now, —"twe-twea-twe-e-e-a," with a peculiar summer languor and plaintiveness, and issuing from the lower branches and growths. Presently we—for I have been joined by a companion—discover the bird, a male, insecting in the top of a newly fallen hemlock. The black, white, and blue of his uniform are seen at a glance. His movements are quite slow compared with some of the warblers. If he will only betray the locality of that little domicile where his plainly clad mate is evidently sitting, it is all we will ask of him. But this he seems in no wise disposed to do. Here and there, and up and down, we follow him, often losing him, and as often refinding him by his song; but the clew to his nest, how shall we get it? Does he never go home to see how things are getting on, or to see if his presence is not needed, or to take madam a morsel of food? No doubt he keeps within earshot, and a cry of distress or alarm from the mother bird would bring him to the spot in an instant.

Despairing of finding the nest of this elusive male, we pushed on through the woods to try our luck elsewhere. Before long, just as we were about to plunge down a hill into a dense, swampy part of the woods, we discovered a pair of birds we were in quest of. They had food in their beaks, and, as we paused, showed great signs of alarm, indicating that the nest was in the immediate vicinity. This was enough. We would pause here and find this nest, anyhow. So we doggedly crouched down and watched them, and they watched us. It was diamond cut diamond. But as we felt constrained in our movements, desiring, if possible, to keep so quiet that the birds would, after a while, see in us only two harmless stumps or prostrate logs, we had much the worst of it. The mosquitoes were quite taken with our quiet, and knew us from logs and stumps in a moment. Neither were the birds deceived, not even when we tried the Indian's tactics, and plumed ourselves with green branches.

Quite near us they would come at times, between us and the nest, eyeing us so sharply. Then they would move off, and apparently try to forget our presence. Was it to deceive us, or to persuade himself and mate that there was no serious cause for alarm, that the male would now and then strike up in full song and move off to some distance through the trees?

After a time I felt sure I knew within a few feet where

A black-throated blue warbler

the nest was concealed. Indeed, I thought I knew the identical bush. Then the birds approached each other again and grew very confidential about another locality some rods below. This puzzled us, and, seeing the whole afternoon might be spent in this manner, and the mystery unsolved, we determined to change our tactics and institute a thorough search of the locality. This procedure soon brought things to a crisis, for, as my companion clambered over a log by a little hemlock, a few yards from where we had been sitting, with a cry of alarm out sprang the young birds from their nest in the hemlock, and, scampering and fluttering over the leaves, disappeared in different directions. [This brought the parent birds on the scene in an agony of distress. Feigning to be disabled, both male and female trailed their plumage on the dry leaves with a helpless, fluttering motion to distract the attention of the intruders from the helpless young and try to decoy them from the scene of the nest.]

The nest was built in the fork of the little hemlock, about fifteen inches from the ground, and was a thick, firm structure, composed of the finer material of the woods, with a lining of very delicate roots or rootlets.

Defunct birds'-nests are easy to find; when the leaves fall, then they are in every bush and tree, and one wonders how he missed them; but a live nest, how it eludes one!

Going a-fishing or a-berrying is a good introduction to the haunts of the birds, and to their nesting-places. You put forth your hand for the berries, and there is a nest; or your tread by the creeks starts the sandpiper or the water-thrush from the ground where its eggs are concealed, or some shy wood-warbler from a bush. One day, fishing down a deep wooded gorge, my hook caught on a limb overhead, and on pulling it down I found I had missed my trout, but had caught a hummingbird's nest. It was saddled on the limb as nicely as if it had been a grown part of it.

Nests least concealed are often concealed the most. Day after day I had searched through my orchard for a king-bird's nest which I knew from the action of the birds and their constant presence there was in one of the apple or pear trees. I looked them all over in vain, time after time. Then I lay down in the grass under one of the tall trees and kept my eyes on the birds. It was a warm, ripe mid-summer afternoon and the fragrance of the world of grass about me and the repose of nature on all sides fairly drowsed my senses. I took a languid interest in watching the two birds and seeing them climb high in the air, now and then, and overtake some bug or beetle that was venturing forth for a pleasure flight in the upper regions of

A kingbird's nest

the air, and then pitch down with their prey in their beaks.

I became so interested in these aerial excursions of the two birds and the lumbering, slow-moving insects that they were picking out of the air, that I quite forgot the nest. After a while, casually turning my head to one side to rest my eyes, I saw the nest on a branch not twenty feet away from me. The thicker foliage and the closer branches of the near-by pear trees offered much more concealment, and upon these I had fixed my scrutiny, and had only run my eye hurriedly over the more open branches of the apple-trees. But there was the nest near the end of a long, low, horizontal branch, with no screen of foliage, and likely to escape the attention on this very account.

A chickadee had a nest somewhere in the old orchard [at Woodchuck Lodge] but we failed to find it. Several mornings in succession she came upon the veranda and filled her beak with the long woolen nap from my steamer rug. She was very bold, as chickadees usually are, and did not mind a bit my standing a few feet away and upbraiding her.

"You are not a good neighbor," I said—"robbing my bed to furnish your own."

She only kept her beadlike eyes upon me and went on with the pilfering. She made a very pretty appearance with her beak filled with the yellow, green, and black wool—a nest-lining, I venture to say, that she had never had before. Each time she disappeared around the corner of the house into the orchard so quickly that my eye failed to follow her. I only hope that her brood throve and that she will come back next summer to help herself to my supply of wool.

[In his book *Far and Near* he tells of an experience he had one July in finding a nest he had long searched for—that of the Louisiana waterthrush or water-wagtail, a bird that builds its nest by mountain streams.]

The nest of its cousin the oven-bird, called by the old ornithologists the golden-crowned thrush, was familiar to me, as it probably is to most country boys,—a nest partly thrust under the dry leaves upon the ground in the woods, and holding four or five whitish eggs covered with reddish-brown spots. The mother bird is in size less than the sparrow, and in color is a light olive with a speckled breast, and she is the prettiest walker to be seen in the woods.

The water-accentor or wagtail is a much rarer bird, and of a darker olive green. As the color of the oven-bird harmonizes with the dry leaves over which it walks, so the color of the wagtail is in keeping with the dark-veined brooks and forest pools along which it flits and near which it nests.

With me [at Riverby] it is an April bird. When the spice-bush is in bloom along the fringes of the creeks, and the leaves of the adder's-tongue or fawn lily have pierced the mould, I expect to hear the water-thrush. Its song is abrupt, bright, and ringing. It contrasts with its surroundings as does the flower of the bloodroot which you may have seen that day.

The Louisiana is a quick, shy, emphatic bird in its manner. Some birds, such as the true thrushes, impress one as being of a serene, contemplative disposition; there is a kind of harmony and tranquility in all their movements; but the bird I am speaking of is sharp, restless, hurried. Its song is brilliant, its movements quick and decisive. You hear its emphatic chirp, and see it dart swiftly beneath or through the branches that reach out over the creek.

It nests upon the ground, or amid the roots of an upturned tree in the woods near the water that it haunts. Every season for many years I have looked for the nest, but failed to find it till last summer.

My son and I were camping in the Catskills, when one day, as I was slowly making my way down one of those limpid trout streams, I saw a water-thrush dart from out a pile of logs and driftwood that floods had left on the margin of the stream. The bird at once betrayed much anxiety, and I knew the nest was near.

I proceeded carefully to explore the pile of driftwood, and especially the roots of an upturned tree which it held. I went over the mass almost inch by inch several times. There was a little cavern in it, a yard or more deep, where the light was dim; a translucent pool of water formed the floor of it, and kept me from passing its threshold. I suspected the nest was in there amid the roots or broken branches, but my eye failed to detect it.

"I will go on with my fishing," I said, "and return tomorrow and lay siege to this secret."

So on the morrow I returned, and carefully secreted myself on a mossy bank a few yards from the pile of driftwood. Presently the parent bird came with food in its beak, but instantly spying me, though I fancied that in my recumbent position and faded gray clothes I simulated well an old log, she grew alarmed and refused to approach the nest.

She flitted nervously about from point to point, her attention directed to me, and uttering a sharp, chiding note. Soon her mate came, and the two birds flitted about me, peering, attitudinizing, scolding. The mother bird is always the bolder and more demonstrative on such occasions. I was amused at her arts and feints and her sudden fits of alarm. Sometimes she would quickly become silent, and stealthily approach the entrance of the little cavern in the pile of driftwood; then, her fears and suspicions reviving, with emphatic chirps she would try again to penetrate the mystery of that motionless, prostrate form on the bank.

The dead branch of a tree that slanted down to the bed of the stream near me was her favorite perch. Inch by inch she would hop up it, her body moving like a band-master's baton, her notes sharp and emphatic, her wings slightly drooping, meanwhile bringing first one eye and then the other to bear upon the supposed danger.

While she was thus engaging my attention, I saw the male quickly slip into the little cavern with loaded beak, and in a moment reappear. He ran swiftly along the dry pebbles a few yards, and then took to wing, and joined in the cry against me. In a few moments he disappeared, presumably in quest of more food.

The mother, after many feints and passes and false moves, half-fearful of her own rashness, darted into the little cavern also. She soon shot out from it on nimble foot, as had her mate, then took to wing, and to fresh peering and abuse of the strange object on the bank.

The male was soon on the scene again, and after a little flourish, entered the shadow of the cavern as before. Pausing a moment, the female did the same. Evidently their suspicions were beginning to be lulled. In less than

half an hour I felt sure I had the birds' secret,—I had seen
in the recesses of the cavern the exact spot where they
seemed to pause a moment and then turn back.

[The next day, using a fragment of a board to bridge
over the little pool, by getting down on his knees and by
peering into the mass of roots amid the moss and moist
stones, he found, in the dim light of the little cavity, the
nest he had wished so much to see. The five young birds
in it, of grayish slate color, at his approach settled down
in the nest to try to keep out of sight.]

I think one never sees a bird's nest of any kind without
fresh pleasure. It is such a charming secret, and is usually
so well kept by the tree, or bank, or bit of ground that
holds it; and then it is such a dainty and exquisite cradle
or nursery amid its rough and wild surroundings,—a point
so cherished and cared for in the apparently heedless econ-
omy of the fields or woods! When it is a new nest and one
long searched for, the pleasure is of course proportionally
greater.

[Even though one may locate a bird's nest quite by
chance, the delight is no less, as he tells in finding a rare
nest on his walk to Slabsides at West Park.]

A week or two later, [in May] in walking along a secluded, bushy lane leading to the woods, which has been
a favorite walk of mine for more than forty years, I chanced
upon another secret treasure open to the eye of heaven,
which gave me a degree of pleasure greater than any other
single incident which my forty years' acquaintance with
the old lane had brought me. Encircled by the stalks of a
tall-growing weed, I chanced to see upon the ground a
deep, bulky, beautifully formed nest. It was a mass of dry
leaves and grasses, with an unusually deep and smooth
cavity lined with very fine vegetable fibre that looked like
gold thread. Evidently a finished nest, I thought, but it was
empty, and there were no birds about. It did not have the

appearance of a nest that had been "harried," as the Scotch boys say, but of one just the moment finished and waiting for its first egg.

A week later I returned to the place and was delighted to find that it was really a live nest. The setting bird had slipped off on my approach so slyly that I had not seen her. The nest contained four small, delicate white eggs marked with fine black specks on their larger ends. Presently two anxious birds, one of them strikingly marked with yellow, black, white, and blue-gray, appeared in the branches above my head, and began peering nervously down upon me and uttering a faint "sip," "sip." "Warblers," I said; and, as they flitted excitedly about me, I soon recognized the golden-winged warbler—a rare bird in my locality, and one whose nest I had never before seen. "What a pretty coincidence," I said—"the nest of the golden-winged warbler at the foot of a clump of goldenrod, and lined with gold thread!"

The old, neglected farm lane had never before yielded me such a treasure. It was like a page from Audubon or Wilson.

[In conclusion, he has an observation to make to those who go birds'-nesting.]

Love the wood-rose, but leave it on its stalk, hints the poet. So, I say, find a bird's nest, but touch not the eggs. It seems to profane the nest even to touch its contents with the utmost care.

7

Exploring the Delaware

[Love of adventure led John Burroughs to explore the eastern branch of the Delaware River in its upper reaches where, perhaps, no white man had travelled by boat before. The full account of his trip is to be found in his book *Pepacton*.

In a flat-bottomed boat he built himself, and with fishing tackle, some cooking utensils and provisions, blankets, wading boots and rain coat, he set out from Arkville, where he launched his boat in a tributary stream and was soon on the Delaware.]

On the whole, the result of my first day's voyaging was not encouraging. I made barely eight miles, and my ardor was a good deal dampened, to say nothing about my clothing. In mid-afternoon I went to a well-to-do-looking farm-house and got some milk, which I am certain the thrifty housewife skimmed, for its blueness infected my spirits, and I went into camp that night more than half persuaded to abandon the enterprise in the morning.

The loneliness of the river, too, unlike that of the fields and woods, to which I was more accustomed, oppressed me. In the woods things are close to you, and you touch them and seem to interchange something with them; but

73

upon the river, even though it be a narrow and shallow one like this, you are more isolated, farther removed from the soil and its attractions, and an easier prey to the unsocial demons. The long, unpeopled vistas ahead; the still, dark eddies; the endless monotone and soliloquy of the stream; the unheeding rocks basking like monsters along the shore, half out of the water, half in; a solitary heron starting up here and there, as you rounded some point, and flapping disconsolately ahead till lost to view, or standing like a gaunt spectre on the shadowy side of the mountain, his motionless form revealed against the dark green as you passed; the trees and willows and alders that hemmed you in on either side, and hid the fields and the farm-houses and the road that ran near by,—these things and others aided the skimmed milk to cast a gloom over my spirits that argued ill for the success of my undertaking.

Those rubber boots, too, that parboiled my feet and were clogs of lead about them,—whose spirits are elastic enough to endure them? A malediction upon the head of him who invented them! Take your old shoes that will let the water in and let it out again, rather than stand knee deep all day in these extinguishers.

I escaped from the river, that first night, and took to the woods, and profited by the change. In the woods I was at home again, and the bed of hemlock boughs salved my spirits. A cold spring run came down off the mountain, and beside it, underneath birches and hemlocks, I improvised my hearthstone. In sleeping on the ground it is a great advantage to have a back-log; it braces and supports you, and it is a bedfellow that will not grumble when, in the middle of the night, you crowd sharply up against it. It serves to keep in the warmth, also. My berth that night was between two logs that the bark-peelers had stripped ten or more years before. As they had left the bark there, and as hemlock bark makes excellent fuel, I had more reasons than one to be grateful to them.

In the morning I felt much refreshed, and as if the night had tided me over the bar that threatened to stay my progress. If I can steer clear of skimmed milk, I said, I shall now finish the voyage of fifty miles to Hancock with increasing pleasure.

When one breaks camp in the morning, he turns back again and again to see what he has left. Surely, he feels, he has forgotten something; what is it? But it is only his own thoughts and musings he has left, the fragment of his life he has lived there. Where he hung his coat on the tree, where he slept on the boughs, where he made his coffee or broiled his trout over the coals, where he drank again and again at the little brown pool in the spring run, where he looked up into the whispering branches overhead, he has left what he cannot bring away with him.

This branch of the Delaware, so far as I could learn, had never before been descended by a white man in a boat. Rafts of pine and hemlock timber are run down on the spring and fall freshets, but of pleasure seekers in boats I appeared to be the first. Hence my advent was a surprise to most creatures in the water and out. I surprised the cattle in the field, and those ruminating leg-deep in the water turned their heads at my approach, swallowed their unfinished cuds, and scampered off as if they had seen a spectre. I surprised the fish on their spawning beds and feeding grounds; they scattered, as my shadow glided down upon them, like chickens when a hawk appears. I surprised an ancient fisherman seated on a spit of gravelly beach, with his back up stream, and leisurely angling in a deep, still eddy, and mumbling to himself.

As I slid into the circle of his vision his grip on his pole relaxed, his jaw dropped, and he was too bewildered to reply to my salutation for some moments. As I turned a bend in the river I looked back, and saw him hastening away with great precipitation. I presume he had angled there for forty years without having his privacy thus intruded upon. I surprised hawks and herons and kingfishers. I came suddenly upon muskrats, and raced with them down the rifts, they having no time to take to their holes. At one point, as I rounded an elbow in the stream, a black eagle sprang from the top of a dead tree, and flapped hurriedly away. A kingbird gave chase, and disappeared for some moments in the gulf between the great wings of the eagle, and I imagined him seated upon his back delivering his puny blows upon the royal bird. I interrupted two or three minks fishing and hunting along shore. They would dart under the bank when they saw me, then presently thrust out their sharp, weasel-like noses, to see if the danger was imminent. At one point, in a little cove behind the willows, I surprised some school-girls, with skirts amazingly abbreviated, wading and playing in the water. And as much surprised as any, I am sure, was that hard-worked-looking housewife, when I came up from under the bank in front of her house, and with pail in hand appeared at her door and asked for milk, taking the precaution to hint that I had no objection to the yellow scum that is supposed to rise on a fresh article of that kind.

"What kind of milk do you want?"

"The best you have. Give me two quarts of it," I replied.

"What do you want to do with it?" with an anxious tone, as if I might want to blow up something or burn her barn with it.

"Oh, drink it," I answered, as if I frequently put milk to that use.

"Well, I suppose I can get you some;" and she presently reappeared with swimming pail, with those little yellow flakes floating about upon it that one likes to see.

I passed several low dams the second day, but had no trouble. I dismounted and stood upon the apron, and the boat, with plenty of line, came over as lightly as a chip, and swung around in the eddy below like a steed that

John Burroughs in a boat

knows its master. In the afternoon, while I was slowly drifting down a long eddy, the moist southwest wind brought me the welcome odor of strawberries, and running ashore by a meadow, a short distance below, I was soon parting the daisies and filling my cup with the dead-ripe fruit. Berries, be they red, blue, or black, seem like a special providence to the camper-out; they are luxuries he has not counted on, and I prized these accordingly. Later in the day it threatened rain, and I drew up to shore under the shelter of some thick overhanging hemlocks, and proceeded to eat my berries and milk, glad of an excuse not to delay my lunch longer.

While tarrying here I heard young voices up stream, and looking in that direction saw two boys coming down the rapids on rude floats. They were racing along at a lively pace, each with a pole in his hand, dexterously avoiding the rocks and the breakers, and schooling themselves thus early in the duties and perils of the raftsmen. As they saw me one observed to the other,—

"There is the man we saw go by when we were building our floats. If we had known he was coming so far, maybe we could have got him to give us a ride."

They drew near, guided their crafts to shore beside me, and tied up, their poles answering for hawsers. They proved to be Johnny and Denny Dwire, aged ten and twelve. They were friendly boys, and though not a bit bashful were not a bit impertinent. It seems Denny had run away, a day or two before, to his uncle's, five miles above, and Johnny had been after him, and was bringing his prisoner home on a float; and it was hard to tell which was enjoying the fun most, the captor or the captured.

"Why did you run away?" said I to Denny.

"Oh, 'cause," replied he, with an air which said plainly, "The reasons are too numerous to mention."

"Boys, you know, will do so, sometimes," said Johnny, and he smiled upon his brother in a way that made me think they had a very good understanding upon the subject.

They could both swim, yet their floats looked very perilous: three pieces of old plank or slabs, with two cross-pieces and a fragment of a board for a rider, and made without nails or withes.

"In some places," said Johnny, "one plank was here and another off there, but we managed, somehow, to keep atop of them."

"Let's leave our floats here, and ride with him the rest of the way," said one to the other.

"All right; may we, Mister?"

I assented, and we were soon afloat again. How they enjoyed the passage; how smooth it was; how the boat glided along; how quickly she felt the paddle! They admired her much; they praised my steermanship; they praised my fish-pole and all my fixings down to my hateful rubber boots. When we stuck on the rifts, as we did several times, they leaped out quickly with their bare feet and legs, and pushed us off.

"I think," said Johnny, "if you keep her straight and let her have her own way, she will find the deepest water. Don't you, Denny?"

"I think she will," replied Denny; and I found the boys were pretty nearly right.

I tried them on a point of natural history. I had observed, coming along, a great many dead eels lying on the bottom of the river, that I supposed had died from spear wounds. "No," said Johnny, "They are lamper-eels. They die as soon as they have built their nests and laid their eggs."

"Are you sure?"

"That's what they all say, and I know they are lampers."

So I fished one up out of the deep water with my paddle-blade, and examined it; and sure enough it was a lamprey. There was a row of holes along its head, and its ugly suction mouth. I had noticed their nests, too, all along, where the water in the pools shallowed to a few feet and began to hurry toward the rifts: they were low mounds of small stones, as if a bushel or more of large pebbles had been dumped upon the river bottom; occasionally they were so near the surface as to make a big ripple. The eel attaches itself to the stones by its mouth, and thus moves them at will. An old fisherman once told me that a strong man could not pull a large lamprey loose from a rock to which it had attached itself. It fastens to its prey in this way, and sucks the life out.

"The lampers do not all die," said Denny, "because they do not all spawn;" and I observed that the dead ones were all of one size and doubtless of the same age.

My boys went to school part of the time. Did they have a good teacher?

"Good enough for me," said Johnny.

"Good enough for me," echoed Denny.

Just below Bark-a-boom—the name is worth keeping— they left me. I was loath to part with them; their musical voices and their thorough good-fellowship had been very acceptable. With a little persuasion, I think they would have left their home and humble fortunes and gone a-roving with me.

The wind still boded rain, and about four o'clock, announced by deep-toned thunder and portentous clouds, it began to charge down the mountainside in front of me. I ran ashore, covered my traps, and took my way up through an orchard to a quaint little farm-house. But there was not a soul about, outside or in, that I could find, though the door was unfastened; so I went into an open shed with the hens, and lounged upon some straw, while the unloosed floods came down. It was better than boating or fishing. Indeed, there are few summer pleasures to be placed before that of reclining at ease directly under a sloping roof, after toil or travel in the hot sun, and look-ing out into the rain-drenched air and fields.

Soon after the first shock of the storm was over, I stopped at a trout-brook and took a few trout for my sup-per, and about six o'clock thinking that the rain was over, I pushed off, and went floating down into the deepening gloom of the river valley. The mountains, densely wooded from base to summit, shut in the view on every hand. They cut in from the right and from the left, one ahead of the other, matching like the teeth of an enormous trap; the river was caught and bent, but not long detained by them.

Presently I saw the rain creeping slowly over them in my rear, for the wind had changed. I wrapped my rubber coat about my blankets and groceries, and bared my back to the storm. I was getting well soaked and uncomplimen-tary in my remarks on the weather. A saucy cat-bird, near by, flirted and squealed very plainly, "There! there! What did I tell you! what did I tell you! Pretty pickle! pretty pickle! pretty pickle to be in!" But I had been in worse pickles, though if the water had been salt my pickling had been pretty thorough.

Seeing the wind was in the northeast, and that the weather had fairly stolen a march on me, I paddled rapidly to the opposite shore, which was low and pebbly, drew my boat up on a little peninsula, turned her over upon a spot which I cleared of its coarser stone, propped up one end with the seat, and crept beneath. I would now test the virtues of my craft as a roof, and I found she was without flaw, though she was pretty narrow. The tension of her timber was such that the rain upon her bottom made a low, musical hum.

When bed-time arrived I found undressing a little awkward, my berth was so low; there was plenty of room in the aisle, and the other passengers were nowhere to be seen, but I did not venture out. It rained nearly all night. When I arose, I had a delicious bath in the sweet, swift-running current, and turned my thoughts toward breakfast.

The making of the coffee was the only serious problem. With everything soaked and a fine rain still falling, how shall one build a fire? I made my way to a little island above in quest of drift-wood. Before I had found the wood I chanced upon another patch of delicious wild strawberries, and took an appetizer of them out of hand. Presently I picked up a yellow birch stick the size of my arm. The wood was decayed, but the bark was perfect. I broke it in two, punched out the rotten wood, and had the bark intact. The fatty or resinous substance of this bark preserves it, and makes it excellent kindling. With some seasoned twigs and a scrap of paper I soon had a fire going that answered my every purpose. More berries were picked while the coffee was brewing, and the breakfast was a success.

The camper-out often finds himself in what seems a distressing predicament to people seated in their snug, well-ordered houses; but there is often a real satisfaction when things come to their worst—a satisfaction in seeing what a small matter it is, after all; that one is really neither sugar nor salt, to be afraid of the wet; and that life is just as well worth living beneath a scow or a dug-out as beneath the highest and broadest roof in Christendom.

By ten o'clock it became necessary to move, on account of the rise of the water, and as the rain had abated I picked up and continued my journey. At several points I saw rafts of hemlock lumber tied to the shore, ready to take advantage of the first freshet. Rafting is an important industry for a hundred miles or more along the Delaware. The lumbermen sometimes take their families or friends, and have a jollification all the way to Trenton or to Philadelphia. In some places the speed is very great, almost equaling that of an express train. The raft is guided by two immense oars, one before and one behind. I frequently saw these huge implements in the drift-wood along shore, suggesting some colossal race of men.

At the East Branch the Big Beaver Kill joins the Delaware, almost doubling its volume. Here I struck the railroad, the forlorn Midland, and here another set of men and manners cropped out—what may be called the railroad conglomerate overlying this mountain freestone.

"Where did you steal that boat?" and "What you running away for?" greeted me from a handcar that went by.

I paused for some time and watched the fish hawks, of which there were nearly a dozen sailing about above the junction of the two streams, squealing and diving, and occasionally striking a fish on the rifts. I am convinced that the fishhawk sometimes feeds on the wing. I saw him do it on this and on another occasion. He raises himself by a peculiar motion, and brings his head and his talons together, and apparently takes a bite of a fish. While doing this his flight presents a sharply undulating line; at the crest of each rise the morsel is taken.

In a long, deep eddy under the west shore I came upon a brood of wild ducks, the hooded merganser. The young were about half grown, but of course entirely destitute of plumage. They started off at great speed, kicking the water into foam behind them, the mother duck keeping upon their flank and rear. Near the outlet of the pool I saw them go ashore, and I expected they would conceal themselves in the woods; but as I drew near the place they came out, and I saw by their motions they were going to make a rush by me up stream. At a signal from the old one, on they came, and passed within a few feet of me.

It was almost incredible, the speed they made. Their pink feet were like swiftly revolving wheels placed a little to the rear; their breasts just skimmed the surface. They had no need of wings; even the mother bird did not use

Fishhawk

hers; a steamboat could hardly have kept up with them. I dropped my paddle and cheered. They kept the race up for a long distance, and I saw them making a fresh spurt as I entered upon the rift and dropped quickly out of sight.

I passed Partridge Island—which is or used to be the name of a post-office—unwittingly, and encamped for the night on an island near Hawk's Point. I slept in my boat on the beach, and in the morning my locks were literally wet with the dews of the night, and my blankets too; so I waited for the sun to dry them. As I was gathering drift-wood for a fire, a voice came over the shadows of the east shore: "Seems to me you lay abed pretty late!"

"I call this early," I rejoined, glancing at the sun.

"Wall, it may be airly in the forenoon, but it ain't very airly in the mornin';" a distinction I was forced to admit.

My voyage ended that forenoon at Hancock, and was crowned by a few idyllic days with some friends in their cottage in the woods by Lake Oquaga, a body of crystal water on the hills near Deposit, and a haven as peaceful and perfect as voyager ever came to port in.

[He shipped the boat home by rail, and later he and his son used it on the Shattega, the stream near Slabsides.]

8

Bird Neighbors at Slabsides

[At Slabsides, the cabin he built in a woodland near his home at West Park, he had the chance to watch a number of birds nesting, among them a pair of chickadees.]

Chickadees rear only one brood in a season. They are properly wood-birds, but the groves and orchards know them also. Did they come near my cabin for better protection, or did they chance to find a little cavity in a tree that suited them? Branch-builders and ground-builders are easily accommodated, but the chickadee must find a cavity, and a small one at that. The woodpeckers make a cavity when a suitable trunk or branch is found, but the chickadee, with its small, sharp beak, rarely does so; it usually smoothes and deepens one already formed.

This a pair did a few yards from my cabin. The opening was into the heart of a little sassafras, about four feet from the ground. Day after day the birds took turns in deepening and enlarging the cavity: a soft, gentle hammering for a few moments in the heart of the little tree, and then the appearance of the worker at the opening, with the chips in his or her, beak. During the preparations for housekeeping the birds were hourly seen and heard, but as soon as the first egg was laid, all this was changed. They

86

suddenly became very shy and quiet. Had it not been for the new egg that was added each day, one would have concluded that they had abandoned the place.

One day a lot of Vassar girls came to visit me, and I led them out to the little sassafras to see the chickadees' nest. The sitting bird kept her place as head after head appeared above the opening to her chamber, and a pair of inquisitive eyes peered down upon her. But I saw that she was getting ready to play her little trick to frighten them away. Presently I heard a faint explosion at the bottom of the cavity, when the peeping girl jerked her head quickly back, with the exclamation, "Why, it spit at me!"

The trick of the bird on such occasions is apparently to draw its breath till its form perceptibly swells, and then give forth a quick, explosive sound like an escaping jet of steam. One involuntarily closes his eyes and jerks back his head. The girls, to their great amusement, provoked the bird into this pretty outburst of her impatience two or three times. But as the ruse failed of its effect the bird did not keep it up, but let the laughing faces gaze till they were satisfied.

The big chimney of my cabin of course attracted the chimney swifts, and as it was not used in summer, two pairs built their nests in it, and we had the muffled thunder of their wings, at all hours of the day and night. One night, when one of the broods was nearly fledged, the nest that held them fell down into the fireplace. Such a din of screeching and chattering as they instantly set up! Neither my dog nor I could sleep. They yelled in chorus, stopping at the end of every half-minute as if upon signal. Now they were all screeching at the top of their voices; then a sudden, dead silence ensued. Then the din began again, to terminate at the instant as before. If they had been long practicing together, they could not have succeeded better. I never before heard the cry of birds so accurately timed.

After a while I got up and put them back up the chimney and stopped up the throat of the flue with newspapers.

The next day one of the parent birds, in bringing food to them, came down the chimney with such force that it passed through the papers and brought up in the fireplace. On capturing it I saw that its throat was distended with food as a chipmunk's cheek with corn, or a boy's pocket with chestnuts. I opened its mandibles, when it ejected a wad of insects as large as a bean. Most of them were much macerated, but there were two house-flies yet alive and but little the worse for their close confinement. They stretched themselves, and walked about upon my hand, enjoying a breath of fresh air once more. It was nearly two hours before the swift again ventured into the chimney with food.

During my first summer here a whip-poor-will used to serenade me every night from a high ledge of rocks in

Slabsides

John Burroughs with His Granddaughter Elizabeth
(Photo by Laura Mackay)

John Burroughs at 25, from a Tintype

Motoring with Mr. and Mrs. Henry Ford, with Edsel Ford at the wheel

With Student-Visitors at Slabsides

At the Foot of Slide Mountain with Elizabeth

A Lesson on the Art of Seeing Things

Examining a Wild Rabbit's Nest

Walking in the Winter Woods

front of my door. At just such a moment in the twilight he would begin, the first to break the stillness. Then the others would follow, till the solitude was vocal with their calls.

One April morning between three and four o'clock, hearing one strike up near my window, I began counting its calls. My neighbor had told me he had heard one call over two hundred times without a break, which seemed to me a big story. But I have a much bigger one to tell. This bird actually laid upon the back of poor Will one thousand and eighty-five blows, with only a barely perceptible pause here and there, as if to catch its breath. Then it stopped about half a minute and began again, uttering this time three hundred and ninety calls, when it paused, flew a little farther away, took up the tale once more, and continued till I fell asleep.

By day the whip-poor-will apparently sits motionless upon the ground. A few times in my walks through the woods I have started one up from almost under my feet. On such occasions the bird's movements suggest those of a bat; its wings make no noise, and it wavers about in an uncertain manner.

The first year of my cabin life a pair of robins attempted to build a nest upon the round timber that forms the plate under my porch roof. But it was a poor place to build in. It took nearly a week's time and caused the birds a great waste of labor to find this out. The coarse material they brought for the foundation would not bed well upon the rounded surface of the timber, and every vagrant breeze that came along swept it off. My porch was kept littered with twigs and weed-stalks for days, till finally the birds abandoned the undertaking. The next season a wiser or more experienced pair made the attempt again, and succeeded. They placed the nest against the rafter where it joins the plate; they used mud from the start to level up and to hold the first twigs and straws, and had soon completed a firm, shapely structure. When the young were about ready to fly, it was interesting to note that there was apparently an older and a younger, as in most families. One bird was more advanced than any of the others.

I happened to be looking at it when the first impulse to get outside the nest seemed to seize it. Its parents were encouraging it with calls and assurances from some rocks a few yards away. It answered their calls in vigorous, strident tones. Then it climbed over the edge of the nest upon the plate, took a few steps forward, then a few more, till it was a yard from the nest and near the end of the timber, and could look off into free space. Its parents apparently shouted, "Come on!" But its courage was not quite equal to the leap; it looked around, and seeing how far it was from home, scampered back to the nest, and climbed into it like a frightened child. It had made its first journey into the world, but the home tie had brought it quickly back.

A few hours afterward it journeyed to the end of the plate again, and then turned and rushed back. The third time its heart was braver, its wings stronger, and leaping into the air with a shout, it flew easily to some rocks a dozen or more yards away. Each of the young in succession, at intervals of nearly a day, left the nest in this manner. There would be the first journey of a few feet along the plate, the first sudden panic at being so far from home, the rush back, a second and perhaps a third attempt, and the irrevocable leap into the air and a clamorous flight to a near-by bush or rock. Young birds never go back when they have once taken flight. The first free flap of the wing severs forever the ties that bind them to home.

[John Burroughs wished to have bluebirds nesting by his cabin too. One weekend when the President's son, Teddy Roosevelt Junior, then twelve years old, was visiting him, they had an adventure while looking for a section of a tree to use for a bluebird house.]

One day in early May, Ted and I made an expedition to the Shattega, a still, dark, deep stream that loiters silently through the woods not far from my cabin. As we paddled along, we were on the alert for any bit of wild life of bird or beast that might turn up. Ted was especially on the lookout for birds'-nests, and many times I pushed the boat up close to the bank that he might explore with his slender arm the cavities the woodpeckers had made in the dead tree trunks that bordered or overhung the stream.

Only once did he bring out a handful of material that suggested a bird's-nest, and on examining it, sure enough, there was a bird's egg, the egg of the chickadee. The boy had clutched the nest, egg and all, and had made such a wreck of the former that we concluded it was useless to try to restore it and return it to the cavity. So Ted added the egg to his collection, and, I suspect, regretted the result of his eager dive into the hollow stub less than I did.

There were so many of these abandoned woodpecker chambers in the small dead trees as we went along that I determined to secure the section of a tree containing a good one to take home and put up for the bluebirds. "Why don't the bluebirds occupy them here?" inquired Ted. "Oh," I replied, "bluebirds do not come so far into the woods as this. They prefer nesting-places in the open, and near human habitations." After carefully scrutinizing several of the trees, we at last saw one that seemed to fill the bill. It was a small dead tree trunk seven or eight inches in diameter, that leaned out over the water, and from which the top had been broken. The hole, round and firm, was ten or twelve feet above us.

After considerable effort I succeeded in breaking the stub off near the ground, and brought it down into the boat. "Just the thing," I said; "surely the bluebirds will prefer this to an artificial box." But, lo and behold, it already had bluebirds in it! We had not heard a sound or seen a feather till the trunk was in our hands, when, on peering into the cavity, we discovered two young bluebirds about half grown. This was a predicament indeed! My venture had proved to be more rash and regrettable than Ted's.

Well, the only thing we could do was to stand the tree trunk up again as well as we could, and as near as we could to where it had stood before. This was no easy thing. But after a time we had it fairly well replaced, one end standing in the mud of the shallow water and the other resting against a tree. This left the hole to the nest about ten feet below and to one side of its former position. Just then we heard the voice of one of the parent birds, and we quickly paddled to the other side of the stream, fifty feet away, to watch her proceedings, saying to each other, "Too bad," "Too bad." The mother bird had a large beetle in her beak. She alighted upon a limb a few feet above the former site of her nest, looked down upon us, uttered a note or two, and then dropped down confidently to the point in the vacant air where the entrance to her nest had been but few moments before.

Here she hovered on the wing a second or two, looking for something that was not there, and then returned to the perch she had just left, apparently not a little disturbed. She hammered the beetle rather excitedly upon the limb a few times, as if it were in some way at fault, then dropped down to try for her nest again. Only vacant air there! She hovers and hovers, her blue wings flickering in the checkered light; surely that precious hole *must* be there; but no, again she is baffled, and again she returns to her perch, and mauls the poor beetle till it must be reduced to a pulp.

Then she makes a third attempt, then a fourth, and a fifth, and a sixth, till she becomes very much excited. "What could have happened? am I dreaming? has that beetle hoodooed me?" she seems to say, and in her dismay she lets the bug drop, and looks bewilderedly about her. Then she flies away through the woods, calling. "Going for her mate," I said to Ted. "She is in deep trouble, and she wants sympathy and help."

In a few minutes we heard her mate answer, and presently the two birds came hurrying to the spot, both with loaded beaks. They perched upon the familiar limb above the site of the nest, and the mate seemed to say, "My dear, what has happened to you? I can find that nest." And he dived down, and brought up in the empty air just as the mother had done. How he winnowed it with his eager wings! how he seemed to bear on to that blank space! His mate sat regarding him intently, confident, I think, that he would find the clew. But he did not. Baffled and excited, he returned to the perch beside her.

Then she tried again, then he rushed down once more, then they both assaulted the place, but it would not give up its secret. They talked, they encouraged each other, and they kept up the search, now one, now the other, now both together. Sometimes they dropped down to within a few feet of the entrance to the nest, and we thought they would surely find it. No, their minds and eyes were intent only upon that square foot of space where the nest had been. Soon they withdrew to a large limb many feet higher up, and seemed to say to themselves, "Well, it is not there, but it must be here somewhere; let us look about."

A few minutes elapsed, when we saw the mother bird spring from her perch and go straight as an arrow to the nest. Her maternal eye had proved the quicker. She had found her young. Something like reason and common-sense had come to her rescue; she had taken time to look about, and behold! there was that precious doorway. She thrust her head into it, then sent back a call to her mate, then went farther in, then withdrew. "Yes, it is true, they are here, they are here!" Then she went in again, gave them the food in her beak, and then gave place to her mate, who, after similar demonstrations of joy, also gave them his morsel.

Ted and I breathed freer. A burden had been taken from our minds and hearts, and we went cheerfully on our way. We had learned something, too; we had learned that when in the deep woods you think of bluebirds, bluebirds may be nearer you than you think.

9

Slide Mountain

[John Burroughs enjoyed hiking. In his book *Fresh Fields* one will find an account of his experiences climbing Ben Venue in Scotland and Helvellyn in the Lake District of England. The following describes his first ascent of Slide, the highest of the Catskill Mountains in New York State. On the summit of Slide there is now a bronze plaque in his honor.]

On looking at the southern and more distant Catskills from the Hudson River on the east, or on looking at them from the west from some point of vantage in Delaware County, you see, amid the group of mountains, one that looks like the back and shoulders of a gigantic horse. The horse has got his head down grazing; the shoulders are high, and the descent from them down his neck very steep; if he were to lift up his head, one sees that it would be carried far above all other peaks, and that the noble beast might gaze straight to his peers in the Adirondacks or the White Mountains.

But the head and neck never come up; some spell or enchantment keeps it down there amid the mighty herd; and the high round shoulders and the smooth strong back of the steed are alone visible. The peak to which I

95

refer is Slide Mountain, the highest of the Catskills by some two hundred feet, and probably the most inaccessible; certainly the hardest to get a view of, it is hedged about so completely by other peaks—the greatest mountain of them all, and apparently the least willing to be seen; only at a distance of thirty or forty miles is it seen to stand up above all other peaks. It takes its name from a landslide which occurred many years ago down its steep northern side, or down the neck of the grazing steed. The mane of spruce and balsam fir was stripped away for many hundred feet, leaving a long gray streak visible from afar.

This mountain had been a challenge to me for many years. I had camped in the wilderness on all sides of it, and whenever I had caught a glimpse of its summit I had promised myself to set foot there before another season passed. But the seasons came and went, and my feet got no nimbler and Slide Mountain no lower, until finally one June, reinforced by three other climbers, I determined upon the ascent and upon making it from the most difficult side.

We had been told of parties who had essayed the ascent from this side, and had returned baffled and bewildered. In a tangle of primitive woods, the very bigness of the mountain baffles one. It is all mountain; whichever way you turn—and one turns sometimes in such cases before he knows it—the foot finds a steep and rugged ascent.

The eye is of little service; one must be sure of his bearings and push boldly on and up. One is not unlike a flea upon a great shaggy beast, looking for the animal's head; or even like a much smaller and much less nimble creature—he may waste his time and steps, and think he has reached the head when he is only upon the rump.

We broke camp early in the morning, and with our blankets strapped to our backs and rations in our pockets for two days, set out along an ancient and in places an

obliterated bark road[1] that followed and crossed and re-
crossed the stream. The morning was bright and warm,
but the wind was fitful and petulant, and I predicted rain.
What a forest solitude our obstructed and dilapidated
wood-road led us through! five miles of primitive woods
before we came to the forks, three miles before we came
to the "burnt shanty," a name merely—no shanty there
now for twenty-five years past. The ravages of the bark-
peelers were still visible, now in a space thickly strewn
with the soft and decayed trunks of hemlock-trees, and
overgrown with wild cherry, then in huge mossy logs
scattered through the beech and maple woods; some of
these logs were so soft and mossy that one could sit or
recline upon them as upon a sofa.

At the forks there was a bewildering maze of under-
brush and great trees, and the way did not seem at all
certain, but in assaulting a mountain, as in assaulting a
fort, boldness is the watchword. We pressed forward, following a line of blazed trees for nearly a mile, then, turning to the left, began the ascent of the mountain. It was
steep, hard climbing. We saw numerous marks of both
bears and deer; but no birds, save at long intervals the
winter wren flitting here and there, and darting under
logs and rubbish like a mouse. Occasionally its gushing,
lyrical song would break the silence. After we had climbed
an hour or two, the clouds began to gather, and presently
the rain began to come down. This was discouraging; but
we put our backs up against trees and rocks, and waited
for the shower to pass. But the shower was light and
brief, and we were soon under way again.

---

[1] In the first half of the nineteenth century one of the local in-
dustries was the collecting of bark for use in tanneries. Hemlock
trees were stripped of their bark and left to rot on the ground.
The bark-peelers made wagon roads through the woods so they
could bring their loads of bark to shipping points.

Winter wren

Three hours from the forks brought us out on the broad level back of the mountain upon which Slide, considered as an isolated peak, is reared. After a time we entered a dense growth of spruce which covered a slight depression in the table of the mountain. The moss was deep, the ground spongy, the light dim, the air hushed. The transition from the open, leafy woods to this dim, silent, weird grove was very marked. It was like the passage from the street into the temple. Here we paused awhile and ate our lunch, and refreshed ourselves with water gathered from a little well sunk in the moss.

The quiet and repose of this spruce grove proved to be the calm that goes before the storm. As we passed out of it, we came plump upon the almost perpendicular battlements of Slide. The mountain rose like a huge, rock-bound fortress from this plain-like expanse. It was ledge upon ledge, precipice upon precipice, up which and over which we made our way slowly and with great labor, now pulling ourselves up by our hands, then cautiously finding niches for our feet and zigzagging right and left from shelf to shelf. This northern side of the mountain was thickly covered with moss and lichens, like the north side of a tree. This made it soft to the foot, and broke many a slip and fall. Everywhere a stunted growth of yellow birch, mountain ash, and spruce and fir opposed our progress. The ascent at such an angle with a roll of blankets on your back is not unlike climbing a tree: every limb resists your progress and pushes you back; so that when we at last reached the summit, after twelve or fifteen hundred feet of this sort of work, the fight was about all out of the best of us. It was then nearly two o'clock, so that we had been about seven hours in coming seven miles.

Here on the top of the mountain we overtook spring, which had been gone from the valley nearly a month. Red clover was opening in the valley below, and wild strawberries just ripening; on the summit the yellow birch was just hanging out its catkins, and the claytonia, or spring-beauty, was in bloom. The leaf-buds of the trees were just bursting, making a faint mist of green, which, as the eye swept downward, gradually deepened until it became a dense, massive cloud in the valleys. At the foot of the mountain the clintonia, or northern green lily, and the low shad-bush were showing their berries, but long before the top was reached they were found in bloom. I had never before stood amid blooming claytonia, a flower of April, and looked down upon a field that held ripening strawberries. Every thousand feet elevation seemed to make about ten days' difference in the vegetation, so that the season was a month or more later on the top of the mountain than at its base.

The low, stunted growth of spruce and fir which clothes the top of Slide has been cut away over a small space on

Clintonia flowers

the highest point, laying open the view on nearly all sides. Here we sat down and enjoyed our triumph. We saw the world as the hawk or the balloonist sees it when he is three thousand feet in the air.[2] How soft and flowing all the outlines of the hills and mountains beneath us looked! The forests dropped down and undulated away

---

[2] This was in 1885. No one had yet seen the world from an airplane.

over them, covering them like a carpet. To the east we looked over the near-by Wittenberg range to the Hudson and beyond; to the south, Peak-o'-Moose, with its sharp crest and Table Mountain, with its long level top, were the two conspicuous objects; in the west, Mt. Graham and Double Top, about three thousand eight hundred feet each, arrested the eye; while in our front to the north we looked over the top of Panther Mountain to the multitudinous peaks of the northern Catskills.

All was mountain and forest on every hand. Civilization seemed to have done little more than to have scratched this rough, shaggy surface of the earth here and there. In any such view, the wild, the aboriginal, the geographical greatly predominate. The works of man dwindle, and the original features of the huge globe come out. Every single object or point is dwarfed; the valley of the Hudson is only a wrinkle in the earth's surface. You discover with a feeling of surprise that the great thing is the earth itself, which stretches away on every hand so far beyond your ken.

But when the clouds came down and enveloped us on Slide Mountain, the grandeur, the solemnity, were gone in a twinkling; the portentous-looking clouds proved to be nothing but base fog that wet us and extinguished the world for us. How tame, and prosy and humdrum the scene instantly became! But when the fog lifted, and we looked from under it as from under a just-raised lid, and the eye plunged again like an escaped bird into those vast gulfs of space that opened at our feet, the feeling of grandeur and solemnity quickly came back.

A pleasant task we had in reflooring and reroofing the log-hut, on the summit, with balsam boughs against the night. Plenty of small balsams grew all about, and we soon had a huge pile of their branches in the old hut. What a transformation, this fresh green carpet and our fragrant bed, like the deep-furred robe of some huge animal, wrought in the dingy interior! Two or three things disturbed our sleep. A cup of strong beef-tea taken for supper disturbed mine; then the porcupines kept up such a grunting and chattering near our heads, just on the other side of the log, that sleep was difficult. In my wakeful mood I was a good deal annoyed by a little rabbit that kept whipping in at our dilapidated door and nibbling at our bread and hardtack. He persisted even after the gray of the morning appeared.

Then about four o'clock it began gently to rain. I think I heard the first drop that fell. My companions were all in sound sleep. The rain increased, and gradually the sleepers awoke. It was like the tread of an advancing enemy which every ear had been expecting. The roof over us was of the poorest, and we had no confidence in it. It was made of the thin bark of spruce and balsam, and was full of hollows and depressions. Presently these hollows got full of water, when there was a simultaneous downpour of bigger and lesser rills upon the sleepers beneath. Said sleepers, as one man, sprang up each taking his blanket with him; but by the time some of the party had got themselves stowed away under the adjacent rock, the rain ceased. It was little more than the dissolving of the nightcap of fog which so often hangs about these heights.

With the first appearance of the dawn I had heard a thrush in the scattered trees near the hut—a strain as fine as if blown upon a fairy flute, a suppressed musical whisper from out of the tops of the dark spruces. Probably never did there go up from the top of a great mountain a smaller song to greet the day, albeit it was of the purest harmony. Would the altitude or the situation account for its minor key? Loudness would avail little in such a place. Sounds are not far heard on a mountain-top; they are lost in the abyss of vacant air. But amid these low, dense, dark spruces, which make a sort of canopied privacy of every square rod of ground, what could be more in keeping than this delicate musical whisper? It was but the soft hum of the balsams, interpreted and embodied in a bird's voice.

When one is on a mountain-top, he spends most of the time in looking at the show he has been at such pains to see. About every hour we would ascend the rude lookout to take a fresh observation. With a glass I could see my native hills forty miles away to the northwest. I was now upon the back of the horse, yea, upon the highest point of his shoulders, which had so many times attracted my attention as a boy. We could look along his balsam-covered back to his rump, from which the eye glanced away down into the forests of the Neversink, and on the other hand plump down into the gulf where his head was grazing and drinking. During the day there was a grand procession of thunder-clouds filing along over the northern Catskills, and letting down veils of rain and enveloping them. From such an elevation one has the same view of the clouds that he does from the prairie or the ocean. They do not seem to rest across and to be upborne by the hills, but they emerge out of the dim west, thin and vague, and grow and stand up as they get nearer and roll by him, on a level but invisible highway, huge chariots of wind and storm.

In the afternoon a thick cloud threatened us, but it proved to be the condensation of vapor that announces a cold wave. There was soon a marked fall in the temperature, and as night drew near it became pretty certain that we were going to have a cold time of it. The wind rose, the vapor above us thickened and came nearer, until it began to drive across the summit in slender wraiths, which curled over the brink and shut out the view. We doubled up the bed, making it thicker and more nest-like, and as darkness set in, stowed ourselves into it beneath our blankets. The searching wind found out every crevice about our heads and shoulders, and it was icy cold. Yet we fell asleep.

A thrush struck up again at the first signs of dawn, in spite of the cold; but the scene, shut in by fog, was chill and dreary. We were now not long in squaring an account with Slide, and making ready to leave. Round pellets of snow began to fall, and we came off the mountain on the 10th of June in a November storm and temperature.

10

A Barn-Door Outlook

[When John Burroughs was in his seventies, he fixed up a farmhouse on the side of Old Clump Mountain in the Catskills, near his birthplace, which he used as a summer cottage during his last years. He called it "Woodchuck Lodge." A few hundred yards away, in a small hay-barn, he did most of his writing. The following, from *The Summit of the Years*, tells what he observed there.]

I have a barn-door outlook because I have a hay-barn study, and I chose a hay-barn study because I wanted a barn-door outlook—a wide, near view into fields and woods and orchards where I could be on intimate terms with the wild life about me, and with free, open-air nature.

Usually there is nothing small or stingy about a barn-door, and a farmer's haybarn puts only a very thin partition between you and the outside world. Therefore, what could be a more fit place to thresh out dry philosophical subjects than a barnfloor? I have a few such subjects to thresh out, and I thresh them here, turning them over as many times as we used to turn over the oat and rye sheaves in the old days when I wielded the hickory flail with my brothers on this same barn floor.

What a pleasure it is to look back to those autumn days,

generally in September or early October, when we used to thresh out a few bushels of the new crop of rye to be taken to the grist-mill for a fresh supply of flour! How often we paused in our work to munch apples that had been mellowing in the haymow by our side, and look out through the big doorway upon the sunlit meadows and hill-slopes! The sound of the flail is heard in the old barn no more, but in its stead the scratching of a pen and the uneasy stirring of a man seated there behind a big box, threshing out a harvest for a loaf of much less general value.

As I sit here day after day, bending over my work, I get many glimpses of the little rills of wild life that circulate about me. The feature of it that impresses me most is the life of fear that most of the wild creatures lead. They are as alert and cautious as are the picket-lines of opposing armies. Just over the line of stone wall in the orchard a woodchuck comes hesitatingly out of his hole and goes nibbling in the grass not fifty feet away. How alert and watchful he is! Every few moments he sits upright and takes an observation, then resumes his feeding. When I make a slight noise he rushes to the cover of the stone wall. Then, as no danger appears, he climbs to the top of it and looks in my direction. As I move as if to get up, he drops back quietly to his hole.

A chipmunk comes along on the stone wall, hurrying somewhere on an important errand, but changing his course every moment. He runs on the top of the wall, then along its side, then into it and through it and out on the other side, pausing every few seconds and looking and listening, careful not to expose himself long in any one position, really skulking and hiding all along his journey. His enemies are keen and watchful and likely to appear at any moment, and he knows it, not so much by experience as by instinct. His young are timid and

Woodchuck in the field

watchful the first time they emerge from the den into the light of day.

Then a red squirrel comes spinning along. By jerks and nervous, spasmodic spurts he rushes along from cover to cover like a soldier dodging the enemy's bullets. When he discovers me, he pauses, and with one paw on his heart, appears to press a button that lets off a flood of snickering, explosive sounds that seem like ridicule of me and my work. Failing to get any response from me, he presently turns, and, springing from the wall to the bending branch of a near apple-tree, he rushes up and disappears amid the foliage.

Presently I see him on the end of a branch, where he seizes a green apple not yet a third grown, and, darting down to a large horizontal branch, sits up with the apple in his paws and proceeds to chip it up for the pale, unripe seeds at its core, all the time keenly alive to possible dangers that may surround him. What a nervous, hustling, highstrung creature he is—a live wire at all times and places! That pert curl of the end of his tail, as he sits chipping the apple or cutting through the shell of a nut, is expressive of his character. What a contrast his nervous and explosive activity presents to the more sedate and dignified life of the gray squirrel! One of these passed us only a few yards away on our walk in the woods the other day—a long, undulating line of soft gray, silent as a spirit and graceful as a wave on the beach.

A little later, in the fine, slow-falling rain, a rabbit suddenly emerges into my field of vision fifty feet away. How timid and scared she looks! She pauses a moment amid the weeds, then hops a yard or two and pauses again, then passes under the bars and hesitates on the edge of a more open and exposed place immediately in front of me. Here she works her nose, feeling of every current of air, analyzing every scent to see if danger is near. Apparently detecting something suspicious in the currents that drift from my direction, she turns back, pauses again, works her nose as before, then hurries out of my sight.

A highhole alights on the ground in full view in the orchard twenty yards away, and, spying my motionless figure, pauses and regards me long and intently. Finally concluding that I am not dangerous, he stoops to the turf for his beloved ants and other insects, but lifts his head every few seconds to see that no danger is imminent. Not one moment is he off his guard. A hawk may suddenly swoop from the air above, or a four-footed foe approach from any side. I have seen a sharp-shinned hawk pick up a highhole from the turf in a twinkling under just such conditions. What a contrast between the anxious behavior of these wild creatures and the ease and indifference of the grazing cattle!

All the wild creatures evidently regard me with mingled feelings of curiosity and distrust. A song sparrow hops and flirts and attitudinizes and peers at me from the door-sill, wondering if there is any harm in me. A phoebe-bird comes in and flits about, disturbed by my presence. For the third or fourth time this season, I think, she is planning a nest. In June she began one over a window on the porch where I sleep in the open air. She had the foundation laid when I appeared, and was not a little disturbed by my presence, especially in the early morning, when I wanted to sleep and she wanted to work. She let fall some of her mortar upon me, but at least I had no fear of a falling brick. She gradually got used to me and her work was progressing into the moss stage when two women appeared on the porch with brooms. Then Phoebe seemed to say to herself, "This is too much," and she left her unfinished nest and resorted to the empty hay-barn.

Here she built a nest on one of the bark-covered end timbers halfway up the big mow, not being quite as used to barns and the exigencies of haying-times as swallows are, who build their mud nest against the rafters in the peak. She had deposited her eggs, when the haymakers began pitching hay into the space beneath her; sweating, hurrying haymakers do not see or regard the rights or wants of little birds. Like a rising tide the fragrant hay rose and covered the timber and the nest, and crept on up toward the swallow's unfledged family in the peak, but did not quite reach it.

Phoebe and her mate hung about the barn disconsolate for days, and now, ten days later, she is hovering about my open door on the floor below, evidently prospecting for another building-site. I hope she will find me so quiet and my air so friendly that she will choose a niche on the hewn timber over my head. Just this moment I saw her snap up a flying "miller" in the orchard a few rods away. She was compelled to swoop four times before she intercepted that little moth in its unsteady, zigzagging flight. She is an expert at this sort of thing; it is her business to take her game on the wing; but the moths are experts in zigzag flying, and Phoebe missed her mark three times. I heard the snap of her beak at each swoop. It is almost impossible for any insectivorous bird except a flycatcher to take a moth or a butterfly on the wing.

Last year in August the junco, or common snow-bird, came into the big barn and built her nest in the side of a haymow, only a few feet from me. The clean, fragrant hay attracted her as it had attracted me. One would have thought that in a haymow she had nesting material near at hand. But no; her nest-building instincts had to take the old rut; she must bring her own material from without; the haymow was only the mossy bank or the wood-side turf where her species had hidden their nests for untold-generations. She did not weave one spear of the farmer's hay into her nest, but brought in the usual bits of dry grass and weeds and horsehair and shaped the fabric after the old pattern, tucking it well in under the drooping locks of hay. As I sat morning after morning weaving my thoughts together and looking out of the great barn doorway into sunlit fields, the junco wove her straws and horsehairs, and deposited there on three successive days her three exquisite eggs.

Why the bird departed so widely from the usual habits of nest-building of her species, who can tell? I had never before seen a junco's nest except on the ground in remote fields, or in mossy banks by the side of mountain roads. This nest is the finest to be found upon the ground, its usual lining of horsehair makes its interior especially smooth and shapely, and the nest in the haymow showed only a little falling-off, as is usually the case in the second nest of the season. The songs of the birds, the construction of their nests, and the number of their eggs taper off as the season wanes.

The junco impresses me as a fidgety, emphatic, feather-edged sort of bird; the two white quills in its tail which flash out so suddenly on every movement seem to stamp in this impression. My junco was a little nervous at first and showed her white quills, but she soon grew used to my presence, and would alight upon the chair which I kept for callers, and upon my hammock-ropes.

When an artist came to paint my portrait amid such rustic surroundings, the bird only eyed her a little suspiciously at first, and then went forward with her own affairs. One night the wind blew the easel with its canvas over against the haymow where the nest was placed, but the bird was there on her eggs in the morning. Her wild instincts did not desert her in one respect, at least: when I would flush her from the nest she would drop down to the floor and with spread plumage and fluttering movements seek for a moment to decoy me away from the nest, after the habit of most ground-builders. The male came about the barn frequently with three or four other juncos, which I suspect were the first or June brood of the pair, now able to take care of themselves, but still held together by the family instinct, as often happens in the case of some other birds, such as bluebirds and chickadees.

My little mascot hatched all her eggs, and all went well with mother and young until, during my absence of three or four days, some night-prowler, probably a rat, plundered the nest, and the little summer idyl in the heart of the old barn abruptly ended. I saw the juncos no more.

While I was so closely associated with the junco in the old barn I had a good chance to observe her incubating habits. I was surprised at the frequent and long recesses that she took during school-hours. Every hour during the warmest days she was off from ten to twelve minutes, either to take the air or to take a bite, or to let up on the temperature of her eggs, or to have a word with her other family; I am at loss to know which. Toward the end of her term, which was twelve days, and as the days grew cooler, she was not gadding out and in so often, but kept her place three or four hours at a time.

When the young were hatched they seemed mainly fed with insects—spiders or flies gathered off the timbers and clapboards of the inside of the barn. It was a pretty sight to see the mother-bird making the rounds of the barn, running along the timbers, jumping up here and there, and seizing some invisible object, showing the while her white petticoats—as a French girl called that display of white tailfeathers.

Day after day and week after week as I look through the big, open barn-door I see a marsh hawk beating about low over the fields. He, or rather she (for I see by the greater size and browner color that it is the female), moves very slowly and deliberately on level, flexible wing, now over the meadow, now over the oat or millet field, then above the pasture and the swamp, tacking and turning, her eye bent upon the ground, and no doubt sending fear or panic through the heart of many a nibbling mouse or sitting bird. She occasionally hesitates or stops in her flight and drops upon the ground, as if seeking insects or frogs or snakes. I have never yet seen her swoop or strike after the manner of other hawks. It is a pleasure to watch her through the glass and see her make these circuits of the fields on effortless wing, day after day, and strike no bird or other living thing, as if in quest of something she never finds. I never see the male. She has perhaps assigned him

John Burroughs in his barn study

other territory to hunt over. He is smaller, with more blue in his plumage.

One day she had a scrap or a game of some kind with three or four crows on the side of a rocky hill. I think the crows teased and annoyed her. I heard their cawing and saw them pursuing the hawk, and then saw her swoop upon them or turn over in the air beneath them, as if to show them what feats she could do on the wing that were beyond their powers. The crows often made a peculiar guttural cawing and cackling as if they enjoyed the sport, but they were clumsy and awkward enough on the wing compared to the hawk. Time after time she came down upon them from a point high in the air, like a thunderbolt, but never seemed to touch them. Twice I saw her swoop upon them as they sat upon the ground, and the crows called out in half sportive, half protesting tones, as if saying, "That was a little too close; beware!" It was like a skillful swordsman flourishing his weapon about the head of a peasant; but not a feather was touched so far as I could see. It is the only time I ever saw this hawk in a sportive or aggressive mood. I have seen jays tease the sharp-shinned hawk in this way, and escape his retaliating blows by darting into a cedar tree. All the crow tribe, I think, love to badger and mock some of their neighbors.

How much business the crows seem to have apart from hunting their living! I hear their voices in the morning before sun-up, sounding out from different points of the fields and woods, as if every one of them were giving or receiving orders for the day: "Here, Jim, you do this; here, Corvus, you go there, and put that thing through": and Jim caws back a response, and Corvus says, "I'm off this minute." I get the impression that it is convention day or general training day with them. There are voices in all keys of masculinity and femininity. Here and there seems to be one in authority who calls at intervals, "Hawah, haw, haw-ah!" Others utter a strident "Haw!" still others a rapid, feminine call.

Some seem hurrying, others seem at rest, but the landscape is apparently alive with crows carrying out some plan of concerted action. How fond they must be of one another! What boon companions they are! In constant communication, saluting one another from the trees, the ground, the air, watchful of one another's safety, sharing their plunder, uniting against a common enemy, noisy, sportive, predacious, and open and above-board in all their ways and doings—how much character our ebony friend possesses, in how many ways he challenges our admiration!

What a contrast the crow presents to the silent, solitary hawk! The hawks have but two occupations—hunting and soaring; they have no social or tribal relations, and make no show of business as does the crow. The crow does not hide; he seems to crave the utmost publicity; his goings and comings are advertised with all the effectiveness of his strident voice; but all our hawks are silent and stealthy.

Let me return to the red squirrel, because he returns to me hourly. He is the most frisky, diverting, and altogether impish of all our wild creatures. He is a veritable Puck. All the other wild folk that cross my field of vision, or look in upon me here in my fragrant hay-barn study, seem to have but one feeling about me: "What is it? Is it dangerous? Has it any designs upon me?" But my appearance seems to awaken other feelings in the red squirrel. He pauses on the fence or on the rail before me, and goes through a series of antics and poses and hilarious gestures, giving out the while a stream of snickering, staccato sounds that suggest unmistakably that I am a source of mirth and ridicule to him. His gestures and attitudes are all those of mingled mirth, curiosity, defiance, and contempt—seldom those of fear. He comes spinning along on the stone wall in front of me, with those abrupt, nervous pauses every few yards that characterize all his movements. On seeing me he checks his speed, and with depressed tail impels himself along, a few inches at a time, in a series of spasmodic starts and sallies; the hind part of his body flattened, and his legs spread, his head erect and alert, his tail full of kinks and quirks.

When I speak sharply to him, in the midst of his antics, he pauses a moment with uplifted paw, watching me intently, and then with a snicker springs upon a branch of an apple-tree that hangs down near the wall, and disappears amid the foliage. The red squirrel is always actively saucy, aggressively impudent. He peeps in at me through a broken pane in the window and snickers; he strikes up a jig on the stone underpinning twenty feet away and mocks; he darts in and out among the timbers and chatters and giggles; he climbs up over the door, pokes his head in, and lets off a volley; he moves by jerks along the sill a few feet from my head and chirps derisively; he eyes me from points on the wall in front, or from some coign of vantage in the barn, and flings his anger or his contempt upon me.

No other of our wood-folk has such a facile, emotional tail as the red squirrel. It seems as if an electric current were running through it most of the time; it vibrates, it ripples, it curls, it jerks, it arches, it flattens; now it is like a plume in his cap; now it is a cloak around his shoulders; then it is an instrument to point and emphasize his states of emotional excitement; every movement of his body is seconded or reflected in his tail. There seems to be some automatic adjustment between his tail and his vocal machinery.

The tail of the gray squirrel shows to best advantage when he is running over the ground in the woods—and a long, graceful, undulating line of soft silver gray the creature makes! In my part of the country the gray squirrel is more strictly a wood-dweller than the red, and has the grace and elusiveness that belong more especially to the sylvan creatures.

The red squirrel can play a tune and accompany himself. Underneath his strident, nasal snicker you may hear a note in another key, much finer and shriller. Or it is as if the volume of sound was split up into two strains, one proceeding from his throat and the other from his mouth.

If the red squirrels do not have an actual game of tag, they have something so near it that I cannot tell the difference. Just now I see one in hot pursuit of another on the stone wall; both are apparently going at the top of their speed. They make a red streak over the dark-gray stones. When the pursuer seems to overtake the pursued and becomes "It," the race is reversed, and away they go on the back track with the same fleetness of the hunter and the hunted, till things are reversed again. I have seen them engaged in the same game in tree-tops, each one having his innings by turn.

The gray squirrel comes and goes, but the red squirrel we have always with us. He will live where the gray will starve. He is a true American; he has nearly all the national traits—nervous energy, quickness, resourcefulness, pertness, not to say impudence and conceit. He is not altogether lovely or blameless. He makes war on the chipmunk, he is a robber of birds' nests, and is destructive of the orchard fruits. Nearly every man's hand is against him, yet he thrives, and long may he continue to do so!

11

The Art of Seeing Things

[When asked to give talks at schools and colleges, John Burroughs generally chose for his topic "The Art of Seeing Things." It is a subject on which he touched in a number of his essays too. Here are some of his observations on the art of observing things.]

I do not purpose to attempt to tell my reader how to see things, but only to talk about the art of seeing things, as one might talk about the art of poetry, or of painting, or of oratory, without any hope of making one's readers or hearers poets or painters or orators.

The science of anything may be taught or acquired by study; the art of it comes by practice or inspiration. The art of seeing things is not something that may be conveyed in rules and precepts. Some people seem born with eyes in their heads, and others with buttons or painted marbles, and no amount of science can make the one equal to the other in the art of seeing things. There is nothing in which people differ more than in their powers of observation. Some are only half alive to what is going on around them. Others, again, are keenly alive: their intelligence, their powers of recognition, are in full force in eye and ear at all times.

Of course one's powers of observation may be cultivated as well as anything else. The senses of seeing and hearing may be quickened and trained as well as the sense of touch. Blind persons come to be marvelously acute in their powers of touch. Their feet find the path and keep it. They come to know the lay of the land through this sense and recognize the roads and surfaces they have once traveled over. Helen Keller reads your speech by putting her hand upon your lips, and is thrilled by the music of an instrument through the same sense of touch.

So far as seeing things is an art, it is the art of keeping your eyes and ears open. The art of nature is all in the direction of concealment. The birds, the animals, all the wild creatures, for the most part try to elude your observation. The art of the bird is to hide her nest; the art of the game you are after is to make itself invisible. The flower seeks to attract the bee and the moth by its color and perfume, because they are of service to it; but I presume it would hide from the excursionists and the picnickers if it could, because they extirpate it.

Power of attention and a mind sensitive to outward objects, in these lies the secret of seeing things. Can you bring all your faculties to the front, like a house with many faces at the doors and windows; or do you live retired within yourself, shut up in your own meditations? The thinker puts all the powers of his mind in reflection; the observer puts all the powers of his mind in perception; every faculty is directed outward; the whole mind sees through the eye and hears through the ear. If you are occupied with your own thoughts, you may go through a museum of curiosities and observe nothing.

You may know the true observer, not by the big things he sees, but by the little things; and then not by the things he sees with effort and premeditation, but by his effortless, unpremeditated seeing—the quick, spontaneous action of his mind in the presence of natural objects. Anybody can go out with note-book and field glasses and make a dead set at the birds. This does not show powers of observation; it shows only industry and intention. Those who see what others miss, who see quickly and surely, who have the detective eye, like Sherlock Holmes, who "get the drop," so to speak, on every object, who see minutely and who see whole, are rare indeed. The big and exceptional things all can see, but only the true observers take note of the minor facts and incidents.

So few people see discriminatingly and see whole that any testimony, the value of which depends upon accuracy in seeing, needs to be well sifted. Hence the observations of the majority of people are of no scientific value whatever. The following illustrates this point. One spring, being interested in the question as to how the crow picks up a dead fish or other food from the surface of the water—with its feet or its bill, I put the question to the fishermen on the river: Had they ever seen a crow pick up anything from the surface of the water? Oh, yes, lots of times. Did he seize the object with his feet or his beak? They would pause and think, and then some would reply, "Indeed, I can't say; I did not notice." One man said emphatically, "With his feet:" another was quite as sure it was done with the bill.

I myself was sure I had seen crows pick up food from the water, as gulls do, with the bill. I had the vision of that low stooping of the head while the bird was in the act. I asked my son, who spends much time on the river, and who is a keen observer. He had often seen the thing done, but was not certain whether it was with the beak or the feet. A few days later he was on the river, and saw a crow that had spied a fragment of a loaf of bread floating on the water. Having the point in mind, he watched the crow attentively. Down came old crow with extended legs, and my son said to himself, "Yes, he is going to seize it with his feet." But he did not; his legs went down into the water, for what purpose I cannot say, but he seized the bread with his beak, rose up with it and then dropped it, then seized it again in the same way and bore it toward a tree on the shore.

Not many days later I saw a crow pick up something from the river in the same way: the feet went into the water, but the object was seized with the beak. The crow's feet are not talons, and are adapted only to perching and walking. So far as I know, all our birds, except birds of prey, carry their food and their nesting-material in their beaks.

The casual glances or the admiring glances that we cast upon nature do not go very far in making us acquainted with her real ways. Only long and close scrutiny can reveal these to us. The look of appreciation is not enough; the eye must become critical and analytical if we would know the exact truth.

Close scrutiny of an object in nature will nearly always yield some significant fact that our admiring gaze did not take in. I learned a new fact about the teazel the other day by scrutinizing it more closely than I had ever before done; I discovered that the wave of bloom begins in the middle of the head and spreads both ways, up and down, whereas in all other plants known to me with flowering heads or spikes, except the goldenrod and the steeplebush, the wave of bloom begins at the bottom and creeps upward like a flame. In the goldenrod it drops down from branch to branch. In vervain, in blueweed, in Venus' looking-glass, in the mullein, in the evening-primrose, and others, the bloom creeps slowly upward from the bottom.

But with the teazel the flame of bloom is first kindled in the middle; to-day you see the head with this purple zone or girdle about it, and in a day or two you see two purple girdles with an open space between them, and these move, the one up and the other down, till the head stands with a purple base and a purple crown with a broad space of neutral green between them.

This is a sample of the small but significant facts in nature that interest me—exceptional facts that show how nature at times breaks away from a fixed habit, a beaten path, so to speak, and tries a new course.

All things are possible with nature, and these unexpected possibilities or departures from the general plan are very interesting. It is interesting to know that any creature can come into being without a father, but with only a grandfather, yet such is the case. The drone in the hive has no father; the eggs of the unfertilized queen produce drones—that is, in producing males, the male is dispensed with. It is to produce the neuters or the workers that the service of the male is required. The queen bee is developed from one of these neuter eggs, hence her male offspring have only a grandfather.

The close observation of nature, the training of the eye and mind to read her signals, to penetrate her screens, to disentangle her skeins, to catch her significant facts, add greatly to the pleasure of a walk and to life in the country. Natural history is on the wing, and all about us on the foot. It hides in holes, it perches on trees, it runs to cover under the stones and into the stone walls; it soars, it sings, it drums, it calls by day, it barks and prowls and hoots by night.

Explain the matter as we may, the facts of nature are undoubtedly of interest to most persons, and our interest is bound to grow as we enlarge our acquaintance with them,—which is about like saying that our interest keeps pace with our interest. But so it is. Water does not taste good to us until we are thirsty. Before we ask questions we must have questions to ask, and before we have questions to ask we must feel an awakened interest or curiosity. Action and reaction go hand in hand; interest begets

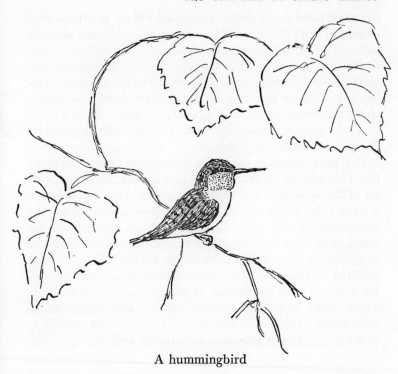

A hummingbird

interest; knowledge breeds knowledge. Once started in pursuit of nature lore, we are pretty sure to keep on. When people ask me, "How shall we teach our children to love nature?" I reply: "Do not try to teach them at all. Just turn them loose in the country and trust to luck." It is time enough to answer children's questions when they are interested enough to ask them.

Knowledge without love does not stick; but if love comes first, knowledge is pretty sure to follow. I do not know how I first got my own love for nature, but I suppose it was because I was born and passed my youth on the farm, and reacted spontaneously to the natural objects about me. I felt a certain privacy and kinship with the woods and fields and streams long before the naturalist awoke to self-consciousness within me. A feeling of companionship with Nature came long prior to any conscious desire for accurate and specific knowledge about her works. I loved the flowers and the wild creatures, as most healthy children do, long before I knew there was such a study as botany or natural history. Nature lore is a mixture of love and knowledge, and it comes more by way of the heart than of the head.

If I were to name the three most precious resources of life, I should say books, friends, and nature; and the greatest of these, at least the most constant and always at hand, is nature. Nature we have always with us, an inexhaustible storehouse of that which moves the heart, appeals to the mind, and fires the imagination,—health to the body, a stimulus to the intellect, and joy to the soul. To the scientist Nature is a storehouse of facts, laws, processes; to the artist she is a storehouse of pictures; to the poet she is a storehouse of images, fancies, a source of inspiration; to the moralist she is a storehouse of precepts and parables; to all she may be a source of knowledge and joy.

12

The Wit of a Duck

The home instinct in birds and animals is one of their most remarkable traits: their strong local attachments and their skill in finding their way back when removed to a distance. It seems at times as if they possessed some extra sense—the home sense—which operates unerringly. I saw this illustrated one spring in the case of a mallard drake.

My son had two ducks, and to mate with them he procured a drake of a neighbor who lived two miles south of us. He brought the drake home in a bag. The bird had no opportunity to see the road along which it was carried, or to get the general direction, except at the time of starting, when the boy carried him a few rods openly.

He was placed with the ducks in a spring run, under a tree in a secluded place on the river slope, about a hundred yards from the highway. The two ducks treated him very contemptuously. It was easy to see that the drake was homesick from the first hour, and he soon left the presence of the scornful ducks.

Then we shut the three in the barn together, and kept them there a day and a night. Still the friendship did not ripen; the ducks and the drake separated the moment we let them out. Left to himself, the drake at once turned his head homeward, and started up the hill for the highway.

Mallard ducks flying

Then we shut the trio up together again for a couple of days, but with the same results as before. There seemed to be but one thought in the mind of the drake, and that was home.

Several times we headed him off and brought him back, till finally on the third or fourth day I said to my son, "If that drake is really bound to go home, he shall have an opportunity to make the trial, and I will go with him to see that he has fair play." We withdrew, and the homesick mallard started up through the currant patch, then through the vineyard toward the highway which he had never seen.

When he reached the fence, he followed it south till he came to the open gate, where he took to the road as confidently as if he knew for a certainty that it would lead him straight to his mate. How eagerly he paddled along, glancing right and left, and increasing his speed at every step! I kept about fifty yards behind him. Presently he met a dog; he paused and eyed the animal for a moment, and then turned to the right along a road which diverged just at that point, and which led to the railroad station. I followed, thinking the drake would soon lose his bearings, and get hopelessly confused in the tangle of roads that converged at the station.

But he seemed to have an exact map of the country in his mind; he soon left the station road, went around a house, through a vineyard, till he struck a stone fence that crossed his course at right angles; this he followed eastward till it was joined by a barbed wire fence, under which he passed and again entered the highway he had first taken. Then down the road he paddled with renewed confidence: under the trees, down a hill, through a grove, over a bridge, up the hill again toward home.

Presently he found his clew cut in two by the railroad track; this was something he had never before seen; he paused, glanced up it, then down it, then at the highway across it, and quickly concluded this last was his course. On he went again, faster and faster.

He had now gone half the distance, and was getting tired. A little pool of water by the roadside caught his eye. Into it he plunged, bathed, drank, preened his plumage for a few moments, and then started homeward again. He knew his home was on the upper side of the road, for he kept his eye bent in that direction, scanning the fields. Twice he stopped, stretched himself up, and scanned the landscape intently; then on again. It seemed as if an invisible cord was attached to him, and he was being pulled down the road.

Just opposite a farm lane which led up to a group of farm buildings, and which did indeed look like his home lane, he paused and seemed to be debating with himself. Two women just then came along; they lifted and flirted their skirts, for it was raining, and this disturbed him again and decided him to take to the farm lane. Up the lane he went, rather doubtingly, I thought.

In a few moments it brought him into a barnyard, where a group of hens caught his eye. Evidently he was on good terms with hens at home, for he made up to these eagerly as if to tell them his troubles; but the hens knew not ducks; they withdrew suspiciously, then assumed a threatening attitude, till one old "dominic" put up her feathers and charged upon him viciously.

Again he tried to make up to them, quacking softly, and again he was repulsed. Then the cattle in the yard

Duck in the barnyard

spied this strange creature and came sniffing toward it, full of curiosity.

The drake quickly concluded he had got into the wrong place, and turned his face southward again. Through the fence he went into a plowed field. Presently another stone fence crossed his path; along this he again turned toward the highway. In a few minutes he found himself in a corner formed by the meeting of two stone fences. Then he turned appealingly to me, uttering the soft note of the mallard. To use his wings never seemed to cross his mind.

Well, I am bound to confess that I helped the drake over the wall, but I sat him down in the road as impartially as I could. How well his pink feet knew the course! How they flew up the road! His green head and white throat fairly twinkled under the long avenue of oaks and chestnuts.

At last we came in sight of the home lane, which led up to the farmhouse one hundred or more yards from the road. I was curious to see if he would recognize the place. At the gate leading into the lane he paused. He had just gone up a lane that looked like that and had been disappointed. What should he do now? Truth compels me to say that he overshot the mark: he kept on hesitatingly along the highway.

It was now nearly night. I felt sure the duck would soon discover his mistake, but I had not time to watch the experiment further. I went around the drake and turned him back. As he neared the lane this time he seemed suddenly to see some familiar landmark, and he rushed up it at the top of his speed. His joy and eagerness were almost pathetic.

I followed close. Into the house yard he rushed with uplifted wings, and fell down almost exhausted by the side of his mate. A half hour later the two were nipping the grass together in the pasture, and he, I have no doubt, was eagerly telling her the story of his adventures.

13

The Pleasures of a Naturalist

The born naturalist is one of the most lucky men in the world. Winter or summer, rain or shine, at home or abroad, walking or riding, his pleasures are always near at hand. The great book of nature is open before him and he has only to turn the leaves.

My morning walk up to the beech wood often brings me new knowledge and new glimpses of nature. This morning I saw a hummingbird taking its bath in the big dewdrops on a small ash-tree. I have seen other birds bathe in the dew or raindrops on tree foliage, but did not before know that the hummer bathed at all.

I also discovered that the webs of the little spiders in the road, when saturated with moisture, as they were from the early fog this morning, exhibit prismatic tints. Every thread of the web was strung with minute spherules of moisture, and they displayed all the tints of the rainbow. In each of them I saw one abutment of a tiny rainbow. When I stepped a pace or two to the other side, I saw the other abutment. Of course I could not see the completed bow in so small an area. These fragments are as unapproachable as the bow in the clouds.

I also saw that where a suspended dewdrop becomes a

jewel, or displays rainbow tints, you can see only one at a time—to the right or left of you. It also is a fragment of a rainbow. Those persons who report beholding a great display of prismatic effects in the foliage of trees, or in the grass after a shower, are not to be credited. You may see the drops glistening in the sun like glass beads, but they will not exhibit prismatic tints. In only one at a time will you see rainbow tints. Change your position, and you may see another, but never a great display of prismatic tints at one time.

How crowded with life every square rod of the fields and woods is, if we look closely enough! Beneath my leafy canopy on the edge of the beech woods where I now and then seek refuge from a hot wave, reclining on a cushion of dry leaves or sitting with my back against a cool, smooth exposure of the out-cropping rock, I am in a mood to give myself up to a day of little things. And the little things soon come trooping or looping along.

I see a green measuring-worm taking the dimensions of the rim of my straw hat which lies on the dry leaves beside me. It humps around it in an aimless sort of way, stopping now and then and rearing up on its hind legs and feeling the vacant space around it as a blind man might hunt for a lost trail. I know what it wants: it is on its travels looking for a place in which to go through that wonderful trans-formation of creeping worm into winged creature. In its higher stage of being it is a little silvery moth, barely an inch across, and, like other moths, has a brief season of life and love, the female depositing its eggs in some suit-able place and then dying or falling a victim to the wood peewee or some other bird. After some minutes of groping and lumping about on my hat and on dry twigs and leaves, it is lost to my sight.

Among the sylvan denizens that next came upon the stage were a hummingbird, a little red newt, and a wood frog. The hummer makes short work of everything: with a flash and a hum it is gone. This one seemed to be exploring the dry twigs for nesting-material, either spiders' webs or bits of lichen. For a brief moment it perched on a twig a few yards from me. My ardent wish could not hold it any longer. Truly a fairy bird, appearing and vanishing like a thought, familiar with the heart of all the flowers and taking no food grosser than their nectar, the winged jewel of the poets, the surprise and delight of all beholders—it came like a burnished meteor into my leafy alcove and was gone as quickly.

All sylvan things have a charm and delicacy of their own, all except the woodchuck; wherever he is, he is of the earth earthy. The wood frog is known only to woodsmen and farm boys. He is a real sylvan frog, as pretty as a bird, the color of the dry leaves, slender and elegant in form and quick and furtive in movement. My feet disturbed one in the bed of dry leaves. Slowly I moved my hand toward him and stroked his back with a twig. If you can tickle a frog's back in any way you put a spell upon him. He becomes quite hypnotized. He was instantly responsive to my passes. He began to swell and foreshorten, and when I used my finger instead of the twig, he puffed up very rapidly, rose up more upon his feet, and bowed his head.

As I continued the titillation he began to give forth broken, subdued croaks, and I wondered if he were going to break out in song. He did not, but he seemed loath to go his way. How different he looked from the dark-colored frogs which in large numbers make a multitudinous croaking and clucking in the little wild pools in spring! He wakes up from his winter nap very early and is in the pools celebrating his nuptials as soon as the ice is off them, and then in two or three days he takes to the open woods and assumes the assimilative coloring of the dry leaves.

The little orange-colored salamander, a most delicate and highly colored little creature, is as harmless as a baby, and about as slow and undecided in its movements. Its cold body seems to like the warmth of your hand. Yet in color it is as rich an orange as the petal of the cardinal flower is rich in scarlet. It seems more than an outside color; it is a glow, and renders the creature almost transparent, an effect as uniform as the radiance of a precious stone. Its little, innocent-looking, three-toed foot, or three and a half toed—how unreptilian it looks through my pocket glass! A baby's hand is not more so. Its throbbing throat, its close-shut mouth, its jet-black eyes with a glint of gold above them—only a close view of these satisfies one.

Here is another remarkable transformation among the small wild folk. In the spring he is a dark, slimy, rather forbidding "lizard" in the pools; now he is more beautiful than the jewel-weed in the woods. This is said to be an immature form, which returns to the ponds and matures the next season; but whether it is the male or the female that assumes this bright hue, or both, I do not know. The coat seems to be its midsummer holiday uniform which is laid aside when it goes back to the marshes to hibernate in the fall.

All this time, behind and above me, concealed by a vase fern, reposed that lovely creature of the twilight, the luna moth, just out of her chrysalis, drying and inflating her wings. I chanced to lift the fern screen, and there was this marvel! Her body was as white and spotless as the snow, and her wings, with their Nile-green hue, as fair and delicate as—well, as only those of a luna moth can be. It is as immaculate as an angel. With a twig I carefully lifted her to the trunk of a maple sapling, where she clung and where I soon left her for the night.

If you "leave no stone unturned" in your walks through the fields, you may perchance discover the abode of one of our solitary bees. Indeed, I have often thought what a chapter of natural history might be written on "Life under a Stone," so many of our smaller creatures take refuge there,—ants, crickets, spiders, wasps, bumble-bees, the soli-

A salamander

tary bee, mice, toads, snakes, newts, etc. What do these things do in a country where there are no stones? A stone makes a good roof, a good shield; it is water-proof and fire-proof, and, until the season becomes too rigorous, frost-proof, too. The field-mouse wants no better place to nest than beneath a large, flat stone, and the bumble-bee is entirely satisfied if she can get possession of his old or abandoned quarters. I have even heard of a swarm of hive bees going under a stone that was elevated a little from the ground.

In the woods one day (it was in November) I turned over a stone that had a very strange-looking creature under it,—a species of salamander I had never before seen. It was five or six inches long, and was black and white in alternate bands. It looked like a creature of the night,—darkness dappled with moonlight,—and so it proved. I wrapped it up in some leaves and took it home in my pocket. By day it would barely move, and could not be stimulated or frightened into any degree of activity; but at night it was alert and wide awake. Of its habits I know little, but it is a pretty and harmless creature. Under another stone was still another species of a dark plum-color, with two rows of bright yellow spots down its back. It evinced more activity than its fellow of the moon-bespattered garb. I have also found the little red newt under stones and several small, dark species.

But to return to the solitary bee. When you go a-hunting of the honey-bee, and are in quest of a specimen among the asters or golden-rod in some remote field, you shall see how much this little native bee resembles her cousin of the social hive. There appear to be several varieties, but the one I have in mind is just the size of the honey-bee, and of the same general form and color, and its manner among the flowers is nearly the same. On close inspection, its color proves to be lighter, while the under side of its abdomen is of a rich bronze. The body is also flatter and less tapering, and the curve inclines upward, rather than downward. You perceive it would be the easiest thing in the world for the bee to sting an enemy perched upon its back. One variety builds its nest in little cavities in rails and posts. But the one with the bronze, or copper, bottom builds under a stone. I discovered its nest one day in this wise: I was lying upon the ground in a field, watching a line of honey-bees to the woods, when my attention was arrested by one of these native bees flying about me in a curious, inquiring way. When it returned the third time, I said, "That bee wants something of me," which proved to be the case, for I was lying upon the entrance to its nest. On my getting up, it alighted and crawled quickly home. I turned over the stone, which was less than a foot across, when the nest was partially exposed. It consisted of four cells, built in succession in a little tunnel that had been excavated in the ground. The cells, which were about three quarters of an inch long and half as far through, were made of sections cut from the leaf of the maple—cut with the mandibles of the bee, which work precisely like shears.

I have seen the bee at work cutting out these pieces. She moves through the leaf like the hand of the tailor through a piece of cloth. When the pattern is detached she rolls it up, and, embracing it with her legs, flies home with it, often appearing to have a bundle disproportionately large. Each cell is made up of a dozen or more pieces; the larger ones, those that form its walls, like the walls of a paper bag, are oblong, and are turned down at one end, so as to form the bottom: not one thickness of leaf merely, but three or four thicknesses, each fragment of leaf lapping over another.

When the cell is completed it is filled about two-thirds full of bee-bread—the color of that in the comb in the hive, but not so dry, and having a sourish smell. Upon this the egg is laid, and upon this the young feed when hatched. Is the paper bag now tied up? No, it is headed up; circular bits of leaves are nicely fitted into it to the number of six or seven. They are cut without pattern or compass, and yet they are all alike, and all exactly fit. Indeed, the construction of this cell or receptacle shows great ingenuity and skill. The bee was, of course, unable to manage a single section of a leaf large enough, when rolled up to form it, and so was obliged to construct it of smaller pieces, such as she could carry, lapping them one over another.

A few days later I saw a smaller species carrying fragments of a yellow autumn leaf under a stone in a cornfield. On examining the place about sundown to see if the bee lodged there, I found her snugly ensconced in a little rude cell that adhered to the under side of the stone.

There was no pollen in it, and I half suspected it was merely a berth in which to pass the night.

The drama of wild life goes on more or less behind screens—a screen of leaves or of grass, or of vines, or of tree-trunks, and only the alert and sympathetic eye penetrates it. The keenest of us see only a mere fraction of it. If one saw one tenth of the significant happenings that take place on his few acres of orchard, lawn, and vineyard in the course of the season, or even of a single week, what a harvest he would have!

14

Wild Life in Winter

December in our climate is the month when Nature finally shuts up house and turns the key. She has been slowly packing up and putting away her things and closing a door and a window here and there all the fall. Now she completes the work and puts up the last bar. To many forms of life in our northern lands, winter means a long sleep; to others it means what it means to many fortunate human beings—travels in warm climes; to still others, who again have their human prototypes, it means a struggle, more or less fierce, to keep soul and body together; while to many insect forms it means death.

Most of the flies and beetles, wasps and hornets, moths, butterflies, and bumblebees die. The grasshoppers all die, with eggs for next season's crop deposited in the ground. Some of the butterflies winter over. The mourning cloak, the first butterfly to be seen in spring, has passed the winter in my "Slabsides." The monarch migrates, probably the only one of our butterflies that does. It is a great flyer. I have seen it in the fall sailing serenely along over the inferno of New York streets. It has crossed the ocean and is spreading over the world. The yellow and black hornets lose heart as autumn comes on, desert their paper nests and

138

die—all but the queen or mother hornet; she hunts out a retreat in the ground and passes the winter beyond the reach of frost. In the spring she comes forth and begins life anew, starting a little cone-shaped paper nest, building a few paper cells, laying an egg in each and thus starting the new colony.

The same is true of the bumblebees; they are the creatures of a summer. In August, when the flowers fail, the colony breaks up, they desert the nest and pick up a precarious subsistence on asters and thistles till the frosts of October cut them off. You may often see, in late September or early October, these tramp bees passing the night or a cold rain-storm on the lee side of a thistle-head. The queen bee alone survives. You never see her playing the vagabond in the fall. At least I never have. She hunts out a retreat in the ground and passes the winter there, doubtless in a torpid state, as she stores no food against the inclement season. In early August of the past year I saw a queen bumblebee quickly enter a small hole on the edge of the road where there was no nest. It was probably her winter quarters.

If one could take the cover off the ground in the fields and woods in winter, or have some magic ointment put upon his eyes that would enable him to see through opaque substances, how many curious and interesting forms of life he would behold in the ground beneath his feet as he took his winter walk—life with the fires banked, so to speak, and just keeping till spring. He would see the field crickets in their galleries in the ground in a dormant state, all their machinery of life brought to a standstill by the cold. He would see the ants in their hills and in their tunnels in decaying trees and logs, as inert as the soil or the wood they inhabit. I have chopped many a handful of the big black ants out of a log upon my woodpile in winter, stiff, but not dead, with the frost, and brought them in by the fire to see their vital forces set going again by the heat. I have brought in the grubs of borers and the big fat grubs of beetles, turned out of their winter beds in old logs by my axe and frozen like ice-cream, and have seen the spark of life rekindle in them on the hearth.

With this added visual power, one would see the wood frogs and the hylas in their winter beds but a few inches beneath the moss and leaf-mould, one here and one there, cold, inert, biding their time. I dug a wood frog out one December and found him not frozen, though the soil around him was full of frost; he was alive but not frisky. A friend of mine once found one in the woods sitting upon the snow one day in early winter. She carried him home with her, and he burrowed in the soil of her flower-pot and came out all right in the spring. What brought him out upon the snow in December one would like to know.

One would see the tree-frogs in the cavities of old trees, wrapped in their winter sleep—which is yet not a sleep, but suspended animation. When the day is warm, or the January thaw comes, I fancy the little frog feels it and stirs in his bed. One would see the warty toads squatted in the soil two or three feet below the surface, in the same way. Probably not till April will the spell which the winter has put upon them be broken. I have seen a toad go into the ground in late fall. He literally elbows his way into it, going down backwards.

Beneath rocks or in cavities at the end of some small hole in the ground, one would see a ball or tangle of garter snakes, or black snakes, or copperheads—dozens of individual snakes of that locality entwined in one many-headed mass, conserving in this united way their animal heat against the cold of winter. One spring my neighbor in the woods discovered such a winter retreat of the copperheads, and, visiting the place many times during the warm April days, he killed about forty snakes, and since that slaughter, the copperheads have been at a premium in our neighborhood.

Here and there, near the fences and along the borders of the wood, these X-ray eyes would see the chipmunk at the end of his deep burrow with his store of nuts or grains, sleeping fitfully but not dormant. The frost does not reach him and his stores are at hand. One which we dug out in late October had nearly four quarts of weed-seeds and cherry-pits. He will hardly be out before March, and then, like his big brother rodent the woodchuck, and other winter sleepers, his fancy will quickly "turn to thoughts of love."

One would see the woodchuck asleep in his burrow, snugly rolled up and living on his own fat. All the hibernating animals that keep up respiration, must have sustenance of some sort—either a store of food at hand or a store of fat in their own bodies, and they come out in the spring lean and hungry. The squirrels are lean the year through, and hence must have a store of food in their dens, as does the chipmunk, or else be more or less active in their search all winter, as is the case with the red and gray squirrels. The fox puts on more or less fat in the fall, because he will need it before spring. His food-supply is very precarious; he may go many days without a morsel. I have known him to be so hungry that he would eat frozen apples and corn which he could not digest. The hare and the rabbit, on the other hand, do not store up fat against a time of need; their food-supply of bark and twigs is constant, no matter how deep the snows. The birds of prey that pass the winter in the north take on a coat of fat in the fall, because their food-supply is so uncertain; the coat of fat is also protection against the cold.

A winter neighbor of mine, in whom I am interested, is a little red owl, whose retreat is in the heart of an old apple-tree just over the fence. Where he keeps himself in spring and summer, I do not know, but late every fall, and at intervals all winter, his hiding-place is discovered by the jays and nuthatches, and proclaimed from the treetops for

A rabbit at Riverby

the space of half an hour or so, with all the powers of voice they can command.

Four times during one winter they called me out to behold this little ogre feigning sleep in his den, sometimes in one apple-tree, sometimes in another. Whenever I heard their cries, I knew my neighbor was being berated.

The birds would take turns at looking in upon him, and uttering their alarm-notes. Every jay within hearing would come to the spot, and at once approach the hole in the trunk or limb, and with a kind of breathless eagerness and excitement take a peep at the owl, and then join the outcry. When I approached they would hastily take a final look, and then withdraw and regard my movements intently.

After accustoming my eye to the faint light of the cavity for a few moments, I could usually make out the owl at the bottom feigning sleep. Feigning, I say, because this is what he really did, as I first discovered one day when I cut into his retreat with an axe. The loud blows and the falling chips did not disturb him at all. When I reached in a stick and pulled him over on his side, leaving one of his wings spread out, he made no attempt to recover himself, but lay among the chips and fragments of decayed wood, like a part of themselves. Indeed, it took a sharp eye to distinguish him.

Not till I had pulled him forth by one wing, rather rudely, did he abandon his trick of simulated sleep or death. Then, like a detected pickpocket, he was suddenly transformed into another creature. His eyes flew wide open, his talons clutched my finger, his ears were depressed, and every motion and look said, "Hands off, at your peril." Finding this game did not work, he soon began to "play 'possum" again. I put a cover over my study woodbox and kept him captive for a week. Look in upon him at any time, night or day, and he was apparently wrapped in the profoundest slumber; but the live mice which I put into his box from time to time found his sleep was easily broken; there would be a sudden rustle in the box, a faint squeak, and then silence. After a week of captivity I gave him his freedom in the full sunshine: no trouble for him to see which way and where to go.

Just at dusk in the winter nights, I often hear his soft

A bluejay and an owl

bur-r-r-r, very pleasing and bell-like. What a furtive, woody sound it is in the winter stillness, so unlike the harsh scream of the hawk! But all the ways of the owl are ways of softness and duskiness. His wings are shod with silence, his plumage is edged with down.

Another owl neighbor of mine, with whom I pass the time of day more frequently than with the last, lives farther away. I pass his castle every night on my way to the post-office, and in winter, if the hour is late enough, am pretty sure to see him standing in his doorway, surveying the passers-by and the landscape through narrow slits in his eyes. For four successive winters now have I observed him. As the twilight begins to deepen, he rises up out of his cavity in the apple-tree, scarcely faster than the moon rises from behind the hill, and sits in the opening, completely framed by its outlines of gray bark and dead wood, and by his protective coloring virtually invisible to every eye that does not know he is there.

The only ones of my winter neighbors that actually rap at my door are the nuthatches and woodpeckers, and these do not know that it is my door. My retreat is covered with the bark of young chestnut-trees, and the birds, I suspect, mistake it for a huge stump that ought to hold fat grubs (there is not even a book-worm inside of it), and their loud rapping often makes me think I have a caller indeed. I place fragments of hickory-nuts in the interstices of the bark, and thus attract the nuthatches; a bone upon my window-sill attracts both nuthatches and the downy woodpecker, and they peep in curiously through the window upon me.

One winter, during four or five weeks of severe weather, several of our winter birds were pensioners upon my bounty—three blue jays, two downy woodpeckers, three chickadees, and one kinglet. I fastened pieces of suet and marrow bones upon the tree in front of my window, then, as I sat at my desk, watched the birds at their free lunch.

The study in snow

Sometimes in my absence a crow would swoop down and
boss the whole crew and carry off the meat. The kinglet
was the least of all—a sort of "hop-o'-my-thumb" bird. He
became quite tame, and one day alighted upon my arm
as I stood leaning against the tree. I could have put my
hand upon him several times. I wonder where the midget
roosted. He was all alone. He liked the fare so well that he
seemed disposed to stop till spring. During one terrible
night of wind and snow and zero temperature I feared he
would be swept away. I thought of him in the middle of
the night, when the violence of the storm kept me from
sleep. Imagine this solitary atom in feathers drifting about
in the great artic out-of-doors and managing to survive. I
fancied him in one of my thick spruces, his head under his
tiny wing, buffeted by wind and snow, his little black feet
clinging to the perch, and wishing that morning would
come.

Last winter and early spring in central Georgia I had
great pleasure in the little glimpses of wild life, mostly
bird-life, that I got from the windows of the cabin study

which my friend built for me in one corner of an old unused building situated in a secluded place near a bushy spring run and a grove of pine- and oak-trees. Many of our more northern birds—such as song sparrows, bluebirds, juncoes, and white-throats—winter in Georgia and impart a sort of spring air to the more secluded places at all times. The mockingbird, the brown thrasher, the cardinal, the meadowlark, the crested titmouse, the Carolina wren, the blue jay, the downy woodpecker, and a few others are there the year round.

The sparrows—white-throats and song sparrows—were at home in the weedy and bushy ground around my little hermitage, and I soon encouraged them to come under my window by a plentiful sprinkling of finely cracked corn and bird-seed. They were always very shy, but they soon learned to associate me with the free lunch, so that, very soon after my appearance—about nine o'clock in the morning—they would begin to gather from the near-by coverts.

In my walk one morning I picked up a cock robin that was unable to fly. As it did not appear to have been injured in any way, and was of very light weight, I concluded it was starving. I took it into the house and let it perch on the back of a chair in the study. It showed little signs of fear and made no effort to escape. I dug a handful of earth-worms, and dangled one of them before its beak. After eyeing it a moment it opened its beak and I dropped the worm into its mouth. Others soon followed, and still others. The bird began to wake up and come to itself. In a little while it was taking the food eagerly and without any signs of fear. I could stroke it with one hand while I fed it with the other. It would sit on my knee or arm and take the food that was offered it. I was kept pretty busy supplying its wants till in the afternoon it began to fly and to run about the room and utter its call-note. Before night it had become so active and so clamorous for its freedom that we opened the window. With a dash and a cry it was out of the house and on the wing to a near-by tree. I trust, with the boost I had given it, it was soon safely on its northward journey.

When one sees the birds in spring scouring about for food where apparently there is no food, or thinks of the mice and squirrels and foxes in the barren, desolate, snow-choked woods, or of the thousands of crows in winter going to and fro night and morning in quest of forage, one realizes how acute and active and discerning they must become to survive at all.